Christian Faith
in Our Time

Christian Faith in Our Time

Rethinking the Church's Theology

PAUL JERSILD

CASCADE *Books* • Eugene, Oregon

CHRISTIAN FAITH IN OUR TIME
Rethinking the Church's Theology

Copyright © 2017 Paul Jersild. All rights reserved. Except for brief quotations in critical publications or reviews, no part of this book may be reproduced in any manner without prior written permission from the publisher. Write: Permissions, Wipf and Stock Publishers, 199 W. 8th Ave., Suite 3, Eugene, OR 97401.

Cascade Books
An Imprint of Wipf and Stock Publishers
199 W. 8th Ave., Suite 3
Eugene, OR 97401

www.wipfandstock.com

PAPERBACK ISBN: 978-1-4982-9586-4
HARDCOVER ISBN: 978-1-4982-9588-8
EBOOK ISBN: 978-1-4982-9587-1

Cataloguing-in-Publication data:

Names: Jersild, Paul.

Title: Christian faith in our time : rethinking the church's theology / Paul Jersild.

Description: Eugene, OR: Cascade Books, 2017. | Includes bibliographical references and index.

Identifiers: ISBN 978-1-4982-9586-4 (paperback) | ISBN 978-1-4982-9588-8 (hardcover) | ISBN 978-1-4982-9587-1 (ebook)

Subjects: LCSH: 1. Postmodernism—Religious aspects—Christianity. | 2. Truth—Religious aspects—Christianity. | 3. Emerging church. | I. Title.

Classification: BR115.P74 J35 2017 (paperback) | CALL NUMBER (ebook)

Manufactured in the U.S.A.   12/13/16

Contents

Acknowledgments | vii
Introduction | ix

Chapter One
Theology and Culture | 1

Chapter Two
Prominent Postmodern Ideas | 9

Chapter Three
Responding to Postmodern Thought | 18

Chapter Four
A Modest Proposal | 27

Chapter Five
The Impossible Necessity: Thinking about God | 38

Chapter Six
On the Reality of God | 50

Chapter Seven
The Historical Jesus | 67

Chapter Eight
The Christ of Faith | 80

Chapter Nine
The Cross and Resurrection | 90

Chapter Ten
New Directions in the Life of the Church | 107

Chapter Eleven
Challenges to Church and Faith | 118

Bibliography | 131
Index | 135

Acknowledgments

In writing this book I have benefited from the support of knowledgeable critics who both share the faith and harbor the concerns that have led to my writing. It all began with four reflection papers written over a six-month period, which I sent to some fifteen friends including theologians, pastors, and laypersons. I told them it was my thinking out loud on a number of issues that had been troubling me in recent years, and that I would appreciate any feedback they might give me. The response was both critical and appreciative, leading me to further reading and reflection and finally to the writing of this book. The overall response convinced me that my concerns were striking a common chord and deserved to be addressed more directly and candidly than they are typically treated within the church.

Of those who have given me valuable assistance I must mention in particular Paul Santmire, whose careful reading of the manuscript has improved it considerably in both style and content. Any inadequacies in those respects lie solely with me.

This work is dedicated to all those who wrestle with matters of faith, who bring their minds as well as hearts to their Christian vocation.

Introduction

During my teaching career I often told my students that Christian theology is a dynamic discipline, changing with the passage of time and responding to the cultural settings in which theologians find themselves. It seemed to be a relatively innocuous truth at the time, one that was obvious enough to anyone familiar with the history of theology. It was also a truth that I felt comfortable in acknowledging as a member of a mainline church (Evangelical Lutheran Church in America) whose theological tradition originated in the sixteenth century, lived through the eighteenth-century Enlightenment, the nineteenth-century Age of Science, and the twentieth-century erosions of secularism.

The truth I affirmed as a matter of course in the mid-twentieth century has taken on more serious dimensions in our own time. The church is encountering a stiff cultural headwind that questions its relevance and even whether it has a viable future. My particular concern in addressing this situation is the church's theology and the role it plays in the image conveyed by the church. Some would say the church's problem is that it presents a medieval theology in a postmodern culture, with predictable results. It is indeed true that the uncritical and widespread understanding of Christian doctrines, in language formulated long ago, is becoming a serious issue for the church. The task of interpreting the faith has become a very challenging matter for theologians today, who are being compelled to rethink the church's tradition in fundamental ways. The need to convey the gospel message in language and concepts that reach the minds and hearts of our contemporaries has become particularly urgent.

A primary concern of mine as a theologian of the church is that laypersons become aware of the theological ferment that prompts this book, and profit from it by the broadening of their own theological horizons. A vital need of the church in every generation is a laity that is theologically literate, and particularly in this postmodern age that need is magnified. One might argue that most of the laity are simply not interested in theology and are content to leave it on the plate of the theologians. That may be true, but that attitude also reflects an earlier, less challenging time for those who profess the faith. There is greater need today to respond in all seriousness to the exhortation of the early church, that each of us "always be prepared to make a defense to anyone who calls you to account for the hope that is in you . . ." (1 Pet 3:15).

I would also hope that writing a book of this kind will prove helpful to those people in the pew who bring questions and doubts about what they understand as Christian teaching. Some of their stumbling blocks may reflect misunderstandings of their own, while others may be unwarranted obstacles posed by common understandings of the theological tradition itself. Given the fact that the Christian tradition now stretches over two millennia, that is hardly a remote possibility. If this work opens them to new insights, fresh understandings, and deeper appreciation of the church's message, it will be my blessing as well as theirs.

So what do I mean by "rethinking" the church's theology? The major issue in my rethinking has to do with the nature of the language we use in talking about God. The dominant image of God in the thinking of Christians is the result of theology uniting itself with philosophy. The result is the God of philosophy or the God of reason, what we call theism or monotheism. It is the omnipotent, omniscient God who rules as a Monarch in a heavenly realm. This is the God of metaphysical reasoning, where God is the Supreme Being at the height of all Being in the universe. It is the God of the Enlightenment who has reigned supreme in the modern era; we can call this God the Supreme Object of our reasoning.

In this dawning postmodern era we are beginning to question—more acutely and forcefully than ever before—the credibility of this metaphysical God. For the Christian it actually involves two questions: does reason have the capacity to comprehend the Mystery that is God, and does the God at which reason arrives—the metaphysical God—hold any particular meaning for Christian faith? To put the question differently, what is the nature of our language concerning a divine reality? Is it descriptive, or at least quasi-descriptive, of God? My thesis is that the ultimate Mystery that is God compels the church in our time to openly acknowledge and emphasize that

Introduction

its faith in a personal God can only be expressed in imaginative language, the language of metaphor and parable. It is the language of Jesus himself.

I will elaborate on this thesis in chapter 4 and following, after the first three chapters in which I address the character of our postmodern age and the response it calls for from Christian theology. The reader may question why I give this much attention to postmodernity, but it is because my thesis assumes that the culture in which the church is planted carries a decisive impact on the language and concepts of the church's theology. I acknowledge that impact in my own thinking, not only as the result of reading the works of postmodern thinkers but perhaps more so, the result of what I have been experiencing and thinking as a child of this age.

My sense is that a fundamental shift in the cultural consciousness of humanity, accentuated in the culture of the West, is now well on its way. One of its dimensions is the movement from a precritical to a critical perspective concerning religious claims. By that I mean that until our era the conventional wisdom assumed a sacred dimension to life, the existence of God, and communication from God through a sacred Scripture. Those assumptions have eroded considerably, until now in this postmodern age we face an overtly secular culture whose disenchantment with religion has become palpable. The church is being challenged to become much more intentional in its response to this situation, which is a daunting task. The first step is to become more attentive to the spirit of the age and its impact upon the thinking and outlook of its inhabitants. That impact, after all, affects believers and non-believers alike. This attentiveness will assist the church in rethinking the language it uses and the claims it makes in communicating the gospel of Jesus Christ.

The feminist theologian Sallie McFague offers a brief description of the postmodern sensibility in terms of the assumptions that define it:

> These assumptions include a greater appreciation for nature; a recognition of the importance of language to human existence; a chastened admiration for technology; an acceptance of the challenge that other religious options present to the Judeo-Christian tradition; an apocalyptic sensibility; a sense of the displacement of the white, Western male and the rise of those dispossessed due to gender, race, or class; and, perhaps most significantly, a growing awareness of the radical interdependence of life at all levels and in every imaginable way.[1]

---

1. McFague, *Metaphorical Theology*, x-xi.

Introduction

The philosopher Albert Borgmann observes that the transition from modernity to postmodernity "is reflected in many kindred shifts of sympathy: from the belief in a manifest destiny to respect for Native American wisdom, from white Anglo-Saxon Protestant hegemony to ethnic pluralism, from male chauvinism to many kinds of feminism, from liberal democratic theory to communitarian reflections, from litigation to mediation, from heroic medical technology to the hospice movement, from industrialism to environmentalism, from hard to soft solutions."[2]

For my purpose I believe it is sufficient to consider some of the leading ideas in postmodern thinking that have a direct bearing on Christian faith and the church's theology (the subject of chapter 2). While these ideas play a role in my rethinking Christian theology, it is not my purpose to present what could be called "a postmodern theology." That would be a much more comprehensive undertaking than what I am doing here. Rather, my purpose is to address the impact of our postmodern consciousness on the way we have traditionally understood some primary Christian teachings, and to lift up alternative ways of understanding those teachings. I will focus particularly on the difference between reason-based philosophy and the kind of theological reflection prompted by Christian faith, including the doctrine of God and interpretations of the incarnation and atonement. I conclude by noting some developments in the life of the contemporary church that resonate with my own thinking about the character and theology of the future church.

A major point of my argument, that imagination and metaphorical language are indispensable in addressing the mysteries of our faith, is nothing new to most theologians. But it is a truth that the church as a whole has not seriously addressed. It poses an urgent task for theologians and laity alike, not only for their own understanding of the church's doctrines but for the sake of a more fruitful communication of the church's message today. I believe the alternative view of church teachings at which I arrive falls within the realm of a responsible orthodoxy, as well as speaking more persuasively to our contemporaries.

Since I am writing primarily for the Christian layperson rather than my academic peers, I have been sparing in my use of notes that cite pertinent texts. Those who want to pursue further reading on topics addressed by this work will find the bibliography at the end of the book helpful. Pursuing this subject of Christian theology in contemporary culture drives home

---

2. Borgmann, *Crossing the Postmodern Divide*, 78.

Introduction

the fact that theology is not a routine, predictable discipline that turns us to the distant past for all of the answers to our theological questions. It is a dynamic enterprise with many surprises and insights along the way because history itself is dynamic and changing, carrying us along to new vistas which shed new light on the faith we profess. In that ongoing journey I hope this volume will make its contribution.

I recently came across a prayer I had copied in a journal I was keeping as a seminary student. To my knowledge its origin is in the country of Kenya. It conveys an authentic expression of Christian faith and theology which is well worth including in a book of this kind, serving as an ideal that summons all of us who would reflect on the nature of our faith.

> From the cowardice that shrinks from new truth,
> From the laziness that is content with half-truths,
> From the arrogance that thinks it knows all truth,
>   O God of Truth, deliver us.

Chapter One

Theology and Culture

We must recognize and acknowledge the fact that there is not and cannot be a gospel which is not culturally embodied. This is simply another way of affirming the historical nature of the gospel.

—Lesslie Newbigin[1]

There is an urgent need today for creative Christian thinkers who will be utterly loyal to the essentials of the biblical gospel, but who will express it in fresh ways appropriate to every culture ... if we are to reach others who are alienated from God and the gospel, [we] will have to enter their cultural worlds, in particular their thought worlds.

—John R. W. Stott[2]

Given the importance of culture to the case I am making, it will be helpful first to consider the nature and impact of culture on our thinking and outlook on life before spelling out the features of my position. This is not a simple matter, however. As a pervasive influence on our thinking about the world and our place in it, culture can be an elusive subject. It not

---

1. Newbigin, *The Gospel in a Pluralist Society*, 189.
2. Stott, cited in McLaren, *Everything Must Change*, 125.

only surrounds us but is inside of us, shaping our thinking, sensitivities, expectations, values, and outlook on life. In particular, the *assumptions* that we imbibe from our culture and that largely define it are often not that apparent. By cultural assumptions I have in mind what is often referred to as a worldview or an outlook on what life is all about. It consists of beliefs about the world one knows and experiences, beliefs that for most people perhaps are more implicit than explicit. Of course, our grasp of the human story and the meaning of life—our sense about what is ultimately real—reflect our personal history. But at the same time, the cultural atmosphere shapes this outlook by establishing limits of plausibility, or what appears to "make sense."

These limits are not arbitrary; they reflect the accumulated experience of one's culture over many years. Christians living in this age of science and technology are not apt to feel comfortable expressing their faith in language and thought patterns of the medieval world or even quite possibly the world of the previous generation. The cultural atmosphere enters into the way we understand and communicate our faith. The language we use, the images and concepts that we are comfortable with in interpreting and communicating our faith, inevitably reflect the cultural world in which we live.

Thus it is no wonder that theologians will often describe their work as "constructive theology," a term that is now preferable to "systematic theology" or "dogmatic theology," terms widely used in the past. It reflects the fact that theologians are continually doing something new because they are interpreting the faith to a changing cultural milieu. To use a common image, they stand with one foot in the ancient world from which their faith emerged and the other in their contemporary world. This poses the challenging task of interpreting the language, concepts, and thought patterns from the one world to that of the other. That ancient world for Christianity is particularly complicated because it includes two quite disparate cultures: the eastern, biblical world of the Hebrews and the western world of the Greeks and Romans where the doctrinal tradition of the church was first formulated. The word we use in referring to this interpretive work is *hermeneutics*, from the Greek word meaning *interpretation*.

Knowledgeable theologians recognize that to proclaim the gospel message is at the same time to interpret it, and the constant question they face is how best to communicate and interpret it in language that both conveys the heart of that message and speaks intelligibly to their contemporaries.

To do this well requires a responsible grasp of the church's tradition as well as sensitive discernment of the times. The tradition itself can place unnecessary obstacles before the laity, who are often puzzled by the language and concepts of that part of the tradition they are most familiar with—the Nicene and Apostolic creeds that they regularly recite in confessing their faith. The Son "begotten" of the Father? Jesus coming "down" from heaven? One may regard such language as quaint or ridiculous, but in either case it calls for interpretation that is seldom offered in the church.

Accommodating vs. Adapting Our Convictions

It is important to recognize that this rethinking and reinterpreting of the church's tradition does not have to mean that we are *accommodating* the gospel to the culture in a way that permits the culture to "water down" or undermine the church's theology. This is a common accusation among conservatives in the church, and it resonates strongly with people who are apprehensive about the changing scene in which they live and what it means for the church. They want the church to be a bulwark *against* change, a refuge from the threats of a secular society. Any suggestion of rethinking the church's teachings is bound to raise red flags for many Christians.

I make a distinction between *accommodating* and *adapting* our Christian convictions to the worldviews that dominate the culture. To *accommodate* those convictions to contemporary thinking would betray a lack of discrimination, an effort to be relevant at all costs. In our scientific age, for example, it would allow the boundaries of acceptable scientific reasoning to unduly influence if not define what is plausible for the claims that theology would make. What we call "modernist theology" that took root in the late nineteenth and early twentieth century is a notable example of theology accommodating itself to a prevailing worldview. The end result was a theology that no longer expressed the heart of the biblical message, with Jesus seen as little more than a teacher of an exalted ethic.

On the other hand, what I mean by *adapting* our theological convictions to contemporary thinking is to recognize that there are always new ways of expressing the genuine meaning of Jesus Christ and the good news that the church proclaims. It will be done differently from one age to another, from one culture to another. This is because theology, if it is alive and well, will recognize prevailing ideas, ideologies, and worldviews that must be addressed, and which, in turn, contribute to the shape and character of theology. Thus the church father Irenaeus in the second century directed his theology to those who denied the goodness of God's creation, a serious threat to the witness of Scripture; and Martin Luther in the sixteenth century addressed a church-dominated culture intent on working its way into heaven; and Karl Barth in the twentieth century engaged the racial ideology and cultural world of the Nazis, speaking a bold word of judgment on human politics and culture. A responsible theology is willing to seriously engage its culture, which means it will inevitably adapt itself to it, reflecting the times in which the theology is written.

Thus the work of theology is never done within a cultural vacuum; its calling is to respond to the culture by the way in which it frames the gospel message, using language and concepts that speak to its contemporaries. In fact, *the vitality and impact of the church's theology are largely dependent on just how successfully it engages its culture.* It demands careful listening to the philosophical, scientific, political, economic, and literary voices of the day, likely bringing both an appreciative and a critical ear to what one is hearing.

The conservative attitude is understandable, but it can harbor the simplistic assumption that if the church is to be true to itself and the gospel it proclaims, it must adhere to the language and concepts that are rooted in the church's tradition and embedded in its creeds from long ago. The temptation is to believe that if Jesus Christ is indeed "the same yesterday, today, and forever" (Heb 13:8), we dare not expect to improve on the language and understandings of the tradition. On the face of it this may appear to be a commonsense view, but it fails to recognize an inexorable truth: history brings change to our understanding and articulation of the faith. If Jesus Christ lives today and not just yesterday, we are obligated to express our faith anew in fresh and creative ways. This task is both a historical imperative and one of the more challenging (as well as rewarding) assignments of the theologian who is intent on supporting the life and mission of the church.

A Historical View

It is not easy for Christians to acknowledge the reality of historical change in their understanding of the gospel message because people tend to assume that a divine truth must be immune to change. And yet, the passing of time is the story of inevitable change to which nothing is immune. A couple of instances from recent church history may help to illustrate this point.

Theology and Culture

In nineteenth-century Europe an emerging historical consciousness gave rise to a new era in Protestant theology. The dominant theologian of the time was Friedrich Schleiermacher (1768–1834), commonly referred to as "the father of modern theology." During his time the books written by theologians were called "dogmatic theology," understood as elaboration on the ancient dogmas of the church. Schleiermacher rejected the notion that was implicit in this practice, that dogma is a timeless version of Christian belief, transcending historical change. He named his major work on theology *Glaubenslehre,* or "teachings of the faith," directed to the church and people of his time and place. This was a revolutionary move and to this day Schleiermacher's interpretation of the faith is regarded suspiciously by defenders of orthodoxy. Yet his theology was a monumental response to the cultural challenges of his time and continues to bring insight to the theological task of our own day.

To cite a more recent example, in 1983 an ecumenical symposium was held in Tübingen, Germany to address the implications for theology of cultural changes associated with postmodernism. The idea of a "paradigm shift" figured prominently in the discussions, a term generated from the ground-breaking book by Thomas Kuhn, a philosopher of science.[3] A dictionary definition of a paradigm is an example, pattern, or model. Kuhn defined the word within a cultural setting as "an entire constellation of beliefs, values, techniques . . . shared by the members of a given community," which he then applied to the scientific community.

One of the conveners of the Tübingen symposium was Hans Küng, a Roman Catholic theologian whose work in many ways has been a call to change and renewal in his church. At the symposium, Küng drew a parallel between physics and theology, citing the paradigms or what he calls "macromodels" that have functioned for each discipline from ancient times to the present. They have served as intellectual frameworks that reflect the cultural milieus of each of the two disciplines and also contribute to them by providing a means of articulation and understanding. In physics he cited the movement from the Ptolemaic to the Copernican to the Newtonian to the Einsteinian eras. In theology he cited the movement from the Greek Alexandrian to the Latin Augustinian tradition in ancient times, from medieval Thomism to sixteenth-century Reformation theology, and finally to

---

3. Kuhn, *The Structure of Scientific Revolutions.*

theology in the modern age, which he called the "critical-interpretative" paradigm that in our time is being challenged.[4]

While Küng acknowledges the obvious differences between the realms of physics and theology, he notes striking similarities in their historical development. In each case it is not a matter of scientists and theologians sitting down and deciding to inaugurate a new age. Rather, it is a response to the fact that the old paradigm in their disciplines was breaking down and was no longer viable. Each of the realities being considered—the physical universe and the gospel tradition—needed new interpretation and understanding in order that the truth might be adequately conveyed. And in each case, Küng observed, there were those scientists and theologians who adamantly resisted changing from the old familiar paradigm to one that was new and unfamiliar. I believe we face that kind of situation today in Christian theology.

Responding to Historical Change

The above two examples of response to historical change are reminders of a salient fact today: we are quite aware of the impact of history on our worldview, our thinking and doing. Particularly since Schleiermacher and another German theologian who followed him, Ernst Troeltsch (1865–1923), both of whom were imbued with a strong historical consciousness, theologians have had to come to terms with this reality. Two opposing responses have been clear: those who defend the philosophical and theological assumptions that govern the ancient formulations of the faith, who demand unswerving allegiance to the language of the creeds and other confessional writings; and those who see the creeds and confessional writings as documents of their time, wielding an important role then but with little claim on our allegiance today. The continuing task of the church from one era to the next is to find a viable position and an appropriate paradigm *between* these two extremes, taking seriously the historical tradition without being wedded to its assumptions and language. That kind of position is what I seek in my rethinking of the church's theology.

Küng raises a pertinent question concerning our acknowledgment of historical change: "Does not theology, even Christian truth itself, faced by nothing but paradigm changes and new conceptions, become a victim of

---

4. Küng and Tracy, eds., *Paradigm Change in Theology*, 10. See also Küng, *Theology for the Third Millennium*, 123–81.

historical relativism, which makes it impossible any longer to perceive the Christian reality and makes every paradigm equally true, equally valid?" In other words, do paradigm changes involve an essential break with what went before, resulting in something entirely new? Küng's answer is a definite "no." The connection of continuity and discontinuity in these historical movements resists any attempt to absolutize any one paradigm or to relativize all of them. For theology the critical issue is *continuity with Jesus Christ*, maintaining the trusting belief in Jesus of Nazareth who is the "Christ of God," the standard for believers "of all time and of all churches."[5]

A participant in this ecumenical gathering, the German theologian Jürgen Moltmann, observed three transitions of fundamental importance that the church is experiencing today and that illustrate ongoing historical change: 1) theology's transition from the denominational to the ecumenical age, in which absolutist claims in behalf of traditional denominational identity are giving way to a sense of the larger, universal church and a common Christian identity; 2) the church's transition from the Eurocentric age (including North America) to the age of humanity as a whole, in which the Christian faith is acquiring new centers of gravity in Africa, Latin America, and Asia with their own distinctive theologies; and 3) the cultural transition from the age of mechanistic domination of the world through science and technology to the age of ecological worldwide community, where we are facing the limits of technological exploitation. All of these developments contribute to a postmodern consciousness and encourage adaptation in the church's theology. Moltmann emphasizes that with this historical evolution the imperative in each era for Christian theology is to "find its Christian identity anew."[6]

It is important to recognize that throughout history the church has always lived with a variety of theological views, reflecting both particular historical circumstances and differences in perspective among individual theologians. That is a reality that will not change in the postmodern age. I am a firm believer that where theology is given free rein, healthy dialogue will enable responsible theology to prevail over theology that is inadequate or irresponsible. That belief is not, I'm afraid, all that persuasive to many church leaders. The slightest deviation in doctrine is often seen as a threat to the stability and well-being of the church. There has to be sufficient confidence in every church establishment to maintain a free and open church,

---

5. Küng and Tracy, eds., *Paradigm Change in Theology*, 30.
6. Ibid., 220–24.

rejecting an authoritarian stance that seeks to control the thinking of its theologians. While some of the ideas in my rethinking theology may strike readers as questionable or provocative, my hope is that they will at least kindle some serious reflection about the doctrinal content of their own faith. That in itself will bring its reward.

Chapter Two

Prominent Postmodern Ideas

Quietly, irrevocably, something enormous has happened to Western humanity. Its outlook on life and the world has changed so radically that in the perspective of history the twentieth century and now the twenty-first are likely to rank— with the fourth century, which witnessed the triumph of Christianity, and the seventeenth, which signaled the dawn of modern science—as one of the very few that have instigated genuinely new epochs in human thought.

—Huston Smith[1]

By the close of the twentieth century, previously fixed systems of thought and behavior had fragmented and the world was understood as radically plural. Equally, Western assumptions about "progress" had been shattered. People had become increasingly suspicious of normative understandings of truth. Socially, radical diversity was increasingly identified as the foundation of human existence.

—Philip Sheldrake[2]

---

1. Smith, *Beyond the Postmodern Mind*, 3.
2. Sheldrake, *Spirituality*, 80.

From a general discussion of culture and our response to it, I need to consider now some of the ideas that are identified with postmodern culture and how they are related to what I am proposing. Whether the contemporary culture is actually a new, postmodern age or a final stage of modernity—a sort of "last gasp" of an expiring culture—has been a topic of lively debate. What is abundantly clear is that the worldview of the modern age, going back to the eighteenth century Age of Enlightenment and shaped by science and technology, is being seriously challenged. Further complicating the picture are those commentators who argue that what we are witnessing is not a transition from one era to another but two "sensibilities" that will continue to coexist indefinitely, each representing a mode of thought that is not likely to end with the closure of a given historical era.[3] However one describes our situation, it is causing significant tensions among Christian theologians today.

My purpose is not to engage the thought of particular postmodern thinkers as such, but to note the influence that some of their ideas have had on theologians who have become serious students of postmodern thought. Modernist theologians, as we shall see, regard postmodern ideas as a very serious threat to Christian theology, while postmodern theologians welcome these same ideas as a promising new direction for theology. It is not surprising that in this time of cultural ferment an increasing number of theologians are seeking a new paradigm or intellectual framework in which to do theology, while others resist that possibility. One can assume that the perspectives of modernity and postmodernity will continue to be argued in western culture for some time to come, and that fact will have a continuing impact on theology as well.

Postmodernism has many different faces, but the writers who have been particularly prominent in articulating it are French thinkers during the mid- to late twentieth century.[4] Their writings both reflect the cultural atmosphere of their time and contribute to it, covering a wide swath of thought and activity. Their attention is focused particularly on the meaning of events and developments occurring in the literary and artistic worlds as well as the realm of philosophy and theology. Prominent among them are Jacques Lacan (1901–81), Roland Barthes (1915–80), Michel Foucault

---

3. Hyman, *The Predicament of Postmodern Theology*, 12–13.

4. For a concise, readable description of postmodern thought, see Butler, *Postmodernism*. For a sympathetic treatment from a theological perspective, see James K. A. Smith, *Who's Afraid of Postmodernism?*

Prominent Postmodern Ideas

(1926–84), Jacques Derrida (1930–2004), and Jean-Francois Lyotard (1924–98). Derrida in particular has addressed theological issues, and though his inclinations run in the direction of atheism his thought has been particularly stimulating to Christian philosophers and theologians. Here are a few postmodern ideas that have entered into theological discussion.

Deconstruction

This term, coming from Derrida, has a negative connotation—"taking apart," or "breaking down." It is a concept that has been widely interpreted, both positively and negatively. The former view sees deconstruction as a promising initiative, leading to reconstruction. It expresses the postmodern wariness about ideas and practices that have become commonplace and immune to question, and the need of a self-critical approach that is willing to question what has been taken for granted. Deconstruction relates not only to the structures of society, to the institutions that shape our common life, but also to the way we think about and experience the world around us. To place under scrutiny the assumptions that shape our experience of the world is a significant exercise; it can be disconcerting and often threatening, or insightful and often liberating.

Christian thinkers have affirmed deconstruction in several ways: as a self-critical principle of reform that is essential to the task of theology,[5] as a fundamentally ethical principle that challenges the status quo on behalf of those on the margins of society,[6] and as an expression of the prophetic spirit exemplified in Jesus himself with encouraging implications for the church.[7] One has to acknowledge, however, that for many postmodern thinkers deconstruction functions as little more than a principle of skepticism, a prominent feature of postmodern thinking.[8] It is common of postmodern ideas that people run with them in different directions, sometimes because of their ambiguity but also because of their fruitful potential.

---

5. Franke, *Manifold Witness*, chapter 11.
6. Smith, *Who's Afraid of Postmodernism?*, 51.
7. Caputo, *What Would Jesus Deconstruct?*, 26–27.
8. This characteristic of deconstructionists draws a considerable amount of criticism. Religion scholar Huston Smith, for example, assails deconstructionists as no more than iconoclasts, people with hammers who are bent on demolition of the western heritage and offering nothing to replace it. See his *Beyond the Postmodern Mind*, 22.

An important part of deconstruction is the view that language is a cultural or social construct. Modernism generally has assumed a realist view of language, meaning that language accurately mirrors the world. The origin of a word's meaning is to be found in the world itself, or reality, an assumption that bestows great confidence in the accuracy or truth of the words we use. Postmodern thinkers question this confidence. Our ability to comprehend what is "out there" is dependent upon the language we use, and we find new words as we search for understanding. As a cultural construct, all language systems carry a certain amount of ambiguity. What meaning a word possesses can only be explained by its relation to other words in the language system, and meanings have a way of gradually changing. Moreover, inherent to every language is a hierarchy of meaning where certain words, such as *God*, *reality*, or *man*, tend to organize and rigidify our thinking in ways that can distort our views of "the way things are," expressing cultural biases that prove to be destructive in many areas of human relationships.

Thus one can see why language is front and center in postmodern thought. The world itself is not accessible apart from language, and it is language that harbors assumptions that contribute to our notions of what is true and right. Deconstruction works to subvert our confidence in what language has led us to take for granted, as well as encouraging its reassessment. We have a strong desire to encapsulate the truth, to reduce and simplify it by putting it in a nutshell, "while everything in deconstruction is turned toward opening, exposure, expansion, and complexification, toward releasing unheard of, undreamt of possibilities *to come*, toward cracking nutshells wherever they appear."[9] One can see how deconstruction opens the gates to challenging the status quo, or what society assumes *ought* to be. This practical (or political) implication of deconstruction is a common feature of postmodern thought, encouraging the prospect of social and institutional change.

Nonfoundationalism

Nonfoundationalism, or antifoundationalism, expresses the opposition of postmodernism to a basic assumption of the modern age going back to Rene Descartes (1596–1650), who is commonly recognized as the father of modern philosophy. Descartes lived during the century following the

---

9. Caputo, ed., *Deconstruction in a Nutshell*, 31.

Prominent Postmodern Ideas

Reformation, which had created a crisis of authority within the church and throughout the western world. In the midst of competing claims concerning philosophical and religious truth, Descartes set out on a quest for certainty, resolving to doubt every belief until he could arrive at a solid, rock-bottom truth. It was a rational quest, leading him to his famous conclusion, *Cogito, ergo sum* ("I think, therefore I am"). The human ego with its rational powers became for Descartes and for the age of modernity the one reliable basis for arriving at knowledge and truth. Reason and logic were identified with knowledge that is both certain and universal, the one foundation for attaining truth that is indubitable. This confidence extended to metaphysical reasoning, including theology and its proofs for the existence of God. This led in turn to a rational, "natural religion" that stood in contrast to the claims of "revealed religion," identified with Christianity.

Postmodern thought repudiates this confidence in reason. The cultural context of our reasoning does not allow for universal claims concerning the truths we arrive at, nor is there a rock-bottom character to the rational conclusions of metaphysical reasoning. Theology is not able to establish rational grounds for the faith it professes. Derrida argues that we never get beyond interpretation in apprehending what is true, a point that applies quite obviously to the realms of philosophy and theology. Interpretation is the result of the limited perspective that characterizes our human situation; we all bring a particular angle to our view of the truth, or reality. Another way of putting it is that you cannot remove the subject from the object being considered.

This point also reflects our dependence on language, which for postmodern thought is the essential mediator for—and, indeed, the prerequisite of—our experience of the world. While the assumptions embedded in language provide a lens by which we can experience and know the world, those assumptions reflect the culture in which we live. This view stands in contrast to the prevailing idea in modernity going back to Jean-Jacques Rousseau (1712–78), who maintained that there are objective, universal truths known directly by reason quite apart from one's culture, religious claims, or any mediating factor such as language.

Hermeneutics of Suspicion

The phrase "hermeneutics of suspicion" was coined by the French thinker Paul Ricoeur, in describing a mode of interpretation characterized by a suspicious attitude toward the subject or thinker being addressed. He was referring to such nineteenth- and twentieth-century thinkers as Karl Marx, Friedrich Nietzsche, and Sigmund Freud, whose thought has had considerable influence on postmodern thinking. The application of this hermeneutic in regard to human reason has been particularly significant. Since the Enlightenment and throughout the modern era, reason has reigned as the crowning feature of humanity, that which distinguishes us from the rest of creation. This positive stance is challenged by the skepticism of postmodern thought, which sees reason as the servant of our motives and purposes that reflect the fallacies and foibles of human nature.

The works of Michel Foucault are a prominent example of this point of view. Foucault sees reason as driven by the quest for power in personal and corporate relationships. It is an instrument of self-interest rather than the benign means by which we determine the truth. Those in positions of authority create rationalist ideologies that justify and maintain their positions of power. Thus the human story is not a grand saga of progress, which the modern age has generally assumed on the basis of the impressive advances of science and technology. Rather, history is the story of one form of domination after the other, reflecting the quest for power that is embedded in the vast web of human relationships.

In his goal of uncovering submerged biases that shape every facet of society, from its social structures to its concept of truth, Foucault is clearly influenced by Friedrich Nietzsche (1844–1900). Nietzsche speaks of the "will to power" that underlies human purposes, focusing primarily on western (Christian) values that he regarded as a cover for motivations that are basically self-serving. While Nietzsche was a lone voice in his own time, in this postmodern era his hermeneutic of suspicion is having considerable impact. When applied to the establishment, or those who wield power in society, it both weakens their position and empowers those on the margins of society whose voices have not been heard or seriously considered by the establishment.

Particularly in regard to the women's movement, this hermeneutical principle has been significant in exposing unexamined assumptions that have maintained patriarchal societies throughout history. It has provided a philosophical basis for the assault on entrenched, discriminatory ideas that have justified the oppression of women. The plight of minority people has also drawn increasing attention in postmodern discussion. Thus the hermeneutics of suspicion has been a contributing factor in the ongoing quest for social justice and equality.

Metanarratives

A significant contribution of Jean-Francois Lyotard to postmodern theory is his argument that "grand narratives" (what are now commonly referred to as "metanarratives") that aim to give meaning to history are no longer credible. These metanarratives see history as progressing toward a desirable end that realizes the goal of history. Examples would include the German philosopher G. W. F. Hegel's interpretation of history as the unfolding of *Geist*, the rational spirit that pervades and guides the course of history; the Marxist belief in a future utopia marked by the liberation of the proletariat and the withering away of the state; the American vision of humanity's emancipation through the spreading of democratic principles rooted in the United States Constitution; and the western confidence in science and technology, promising a more humane world marked by material abundance for everyone.[10]

Lyotard brings a hermeneutic of suspicion to these metanarratives because he sees them as a means of legitimizing the practices, goals, and power of those who promulgate them. These advocates, often politically motivated, seek to bring about the aims and values embodied in the narrative. The all too common result is either a totalitarian development that is coercive and often oppressive, or at least the prescribing of social values that are immune to question.

Christianity also, of course, has a comprehensive view of history, literally from beginning to end—from creation to eschaton. Where it has been politicized in a culture and assumes the character of an imperial religion, it obviously comes under the critique of Lyotard. From their own history as well as that of other religions, Christians by now have good reason to know that uniting religion with politics has been a fateful development, often resulting in tragic forms of oppression that have been utterly contradictory to the teachings of their religion. Ironic as it may be in a supposedly secular age, this joining of religious faith with political power in order to sanction a particular religious vision constitutes a major threat to a civilized world, seen most obviously today in the emergence of "radical Islam." Whatever

---

10. Butler, *Postmodernism*, 13–16.

their origin, whether religious or secular, metanarratives are subject to postmodern suspicion.

Pluralism

The whole direction of postmodern thinking leads to the recognition and affirmation of a pluralistic world. It is a view that recognizes our limitations in arriving at a final or ultimate truth; all that we can discern are many truths that originate from many different sources and contexts. The tremendous diversity in the world, with a plethora of religions and cultures, gives rise to many different truths concerning what is ultimately real.

But pluralism is more than simple diversity; it recognizes that a plurality of truths is being affirmed. Where modernism assumed that reason seeks the one, undivided truth, postmodernism concludes that truth, given its historical character, is inherently plural. There is no arbiter available to tell us which truth is really *the* truth, which means that the notion of "*the* truth" is not a viable idea in the sense that it is accessible to us as rational beings. Where we were once satisfied with relatively simple and straightforward answers that assured us of our possession of *the* truth, we now live in a world with competing ideas concerning every religious, political, and economic issue imaginable, and with no universally convincing answers available. Postmodern thinking captures and affirms this reality.

I will return to the above concepts in various ways in the chapters that follow, bringing both affirmation and critique as I draw out their implications for Christian theology and the life of the church. In doing this I am presenting an example of theology in conversation with its culture, an ongoing task of the church. The postmodern assault on reason in its modern expression has resulted in two tendencies among theologians, one positive and the other negative. The positive response makes a sharp distinction between faith and reason, or faith and theology, emphasizing the priority of faith over theology. It says that what defines the church is not its theology (which is often assumed today) but the faithful life of its members. I embrace that truth, but question the dismissive attitude that it can generate toward the role of theology in the church.

In rethinking the church's theology I am obviously recognizing its importance to the life of the Christian community. Laity who are theologically literate are essential to a church that would make an effective witness in society, and to a church that is alive to the challenges it faces. The critical issue is the expectations we bring to the theological task. Theology is not a rational means of establishing the validity of faith statements, nor does it certify the truth of Christianity in relation to all other religions. To put it more crassly, theology does not divide the saved from the lost. It is, rather, a product of faith and an indispensable means of clarifying, guiding, and nurturing the convictions of believers. With that understanding, an ongoing theological conversation is the mark of a healthy church.

Chapter Three

Responding to Postmodern Thought

Postmodernism can be understood as the erosion of confidence in the rational as sole guarantor and deliverer of truth, coupled with a deep suspicion of science—particularly modern science's pretentious claims to an ultimate theory of everything.... [W]e have not emerged into a radically new postmodern world; rather, our modern world is disrupted and haunted by postmodern suspicions and critique.

—James K. A. Smith[1]

In short, the attitude of doubt that initially led to the construction of new rationalities now leads away again from rationality alone and back to other ways of settling questions of meaning.... [W]e are no longer living in an age where there is a single framework of secular rationality inherently opposed to faith.... What defines the real is no longer as obvious as it once was.

—Guy Collins[2]

---

1. Smith, *Who's Afraid of Postmodernism?*, 62–63.
2. Collins, *Faithful Doubt*, 27.

Responding to Postmodern Thought

There is little prospect of an across-the-board reconciliation between postmodern philosophy and Christian theology, but that is no surprise. Every culture presents a mixture of opportunity and challenge to the church, offering ideas and perspectives that Christian theology can either work with or must repudiate. Thus forging a response to postmodernism requires discrimination in assessing the various themes that characterize its thinking. I believe philosopher Merold Westphal is on target when he maintains that there can and should be appropriations of postmodern thinking on the part of Christians, but with the recognition that postmodern ideas will be "recontextualized" when placed in a Christian setting. This means that not only will there be modifications of postmodern ideas, but that insights from the Christian tradition will bring added depth and meaning to them. We noted this above in several Christian responses to deconstruction. Westphal concludes that there is both "a yes and a no" in the Christian response.[3]

Human Nature

A good example of this "yes and no" from my perspective relates to postmodern insights concerning human nature. The hermeneutics of suspicion, for example, reflects a realistic view of human nature with which Christians can certainly resonate. Christian theology's understanding of sin is self-centeredness, defining our lives in terms of our own self-interests. It is an orientation that turns us away from both God and neighbor, living in opposition to the imperative to love that is central to Jesus' teaching. As Christians we can see the recognition of this self-centeredness in postmodern thinking, where it lifts up the quest for power in human relationships. This quest generates a competitive orientation that can lead quite naturally to domination of the neighbor. This realistic view stands in contrast to the optimism that has generally characterized the modern view of human nature, with its unlimited confidence in our capacity to create a better world. Progress has been regarded as inevitable, usually defined in terms of technological achievements that promise a more humane world.

While there were isolated voices in modernity—harbingers of postmodern thinking—that challenged this sunny optimism, their impact was limited. On the other hand, as we noted, the hermeneutics of suspicion has made a positive contribution in empowering those who suffer from

---

3. Westphal, ed., *Postmodern Philosophy and Christian Thought*, 1–2.

exclusion and marginalization in society. But I'm afraid that even here, the realism in postmodern thought is seriously flawed. It cultivates a pessimism concerning human nature that in many writers is excessive. Michel Foucault, for example, carries his suspicion to such an extreme that it contributes to a thoroughgoing cynicism toward every expression of authority, whether in public or private life. That cynicism has become pervasive in our own country today, encouraging a skeptical attitude in virtually every realm of human activity. In the political arena the impact has been dramatic, eroding the level of trust that is essential to effective government. This lack of trust creates deep rifts that reverberate throughout society, threatening the unity and cohesiveness on which a healthy society depends.

There are other features of postmodern philosophy that raise similar concerns relating to public life. Most of them are rooted in an extreme view of the self. In contrast to the free and self-determining individual of modernism—admittedly also an extreme—the self is seen as a victim, pressed into roles created and governed by centers of power in society. This in turn contributes to a lack of trust among people, particularly toward institutions that govern our political, economic, and religious life. The distrust of universal language and suspicion of global norms and goals also contribute to fragmentation and insecurity, inviting defensiveness and seclusion within one's group or class and a preoccupation with self-protection and self-interest. It is an atmosphere that puts people on edge, where suspicion leads to alienation and conflict.[4] Consequently, while there is a concern for social justice, the skepticism in postmodern thought tends to undermine the obligation to work for the common good, with the sense that "we are all in this together." That sense of unity is the prerequisite to achieving a just society.

Reason

While there are postmodern philosophers whose critique is both too wide and too deep in impugning our rational nature, there is much that can be affirmed. Christian theology has long identified the image of God in human beings with our reason, echoing Greek philosophy in its definition of the human being as the "rational animal." That definition has its validity, but its implications in the modern era since Descartes draw a justified critique. What we have witnessed in modernism is the primacy of reason *in*

---

4. Thiselton, *Interpreting God and the Postmodern Self,* 130–31.

opposition to faith, a human-centered philosophy *in opposition* to theology, a world of science *in opposition* to a world of religion, a world of secularism *in opposition* to the church.[5] We cannot return to a premodern time in order to overcome these dualisms, which would be a fundamentalist dream. Rather, a justified critique would bring a reasoned assessment of the assumptions at work in these dualisms, challenging them on their own grounds. Another substantive critique that postmodern thought brings to the heritage of Descartes's philosophy is its challenge of the absolute confidence in the individual ego as the foundation of a universal reason. Reason in the postmodern view is no guarantee as an avenue to truth, nor can it establish the universality of our judgments. While reason is a major factor in defining the uniqueness of humanity, the postmodern critique can help us to recognize and acknowledge the hard fact that we often are driven to make excessive or mistaken or self-serving claims *on the basis of reason.* This recognition is the self-critical aspect of deconstruction, giving the supposed autonomy of modernity's reason a healthy dose of realism.

The culturally conditioned nature of our reasoning is also part of the postmodern critique that carries positive implications. It is a point that has important consequences for both cultural and political relations in a shrunken world. The colonialism of the nineteenth and twentieth centuries, in which western nations carved up the lands and peoples in eastern and southern hemispheres to serve their own economic and political purposes, was undoubtedly justified in their own minds by the conviction that people from an alien culture and living in poverty must be inferior. From a position of scientific and technological superiority, it was easy for Westerners to regard their culture as inherently superior, a universal, mainstream culture in contrast to the backwater cultures that also inhabited the world. It was a narrow, self-serving attitude that has had devastating historical consequences, leading to alienation and hostility between peoples and nations that are likely to plague the world for generations to come. The culture-centered thinking of postmodernism lifts up the distinctive character of the world's cultures and challenges the cultural chauvinism that has prevailed in the West.

---

5. Küng, *Theology for the Third Millennium*, 197.

Christian Faith in Our Time
Rational and Historical Truth

Modernity's confidence in the universal reach of reason ties in with the assumption that there are universal truths for reason to apprehend. The truth of religions obviously pertains to humanity as a whole, which would make it a claim to universal truth. Thus modernist theologians will accuse postmodernists of undermining the church's gospel by its denial of this fact. Indeed, for many modernists this postmodern position succumbs to nihilism. Postmodern theologians see this complaint as a failure to recognize the pluralism that is inherent to the notion of truth; no one is in a position to discern what is absolutely true for all of humanity. The argument is one that cannot be resolved as long as the assumptions of two competing paradigms govern the scene. But rather than posing an absolute contradiction, I believe there is validity on both sides of this argument. On the one hand we can and should acknowledge the common humanity we share, binding us together as human beings and giving substance to the notion of universal truths. Our faith creates the setting in which our humanity is addressed by the Word of God, a Word for all people.

However, Christians should recognize that this claim is tempered by a number of factors in our encounter with God's Word. Christian faith identifies the Word with Jesus of Nazareth, a historical figure whom we know today as a result of the witness of his contemporaries. A community of faith was established in which Jesus as the Word continued to be proclaimed and interpreted throughout the ages. That Word is appropriated through our finite experience and the lens of many different languages and cultures, giving rise to a wealth of interpretations in claiming the truth of that Word. There is also what we aptly call "the human factor," where fallible minds are at work in transmitting and receiving the truth.

In other words, where we take seriously the impact of the relativities of history, as postmodernism does, we become more aware of the many twists and turns that enter into our faith-claims. When it comes to truths of history, based on things that have happened, those things are quickly blurred and contested. It becomes clear that a most important part of Christian faith is the conviction that the Spirit of God is at work in history; the Spirit brings a message that continues to convict, inspire, nurture, and sustain the human spirit in the midst of historical ambiguities and uncertainties that surround the Word of God.

The believer can react in several ways to this postmodern focus on history and the uncertainties it creates for Christian faith. One way is to simply deny the issue, ignoring the historical complexities embedded in Christian faith (a typical fundamentalist response). Or one can recognize that the very nature of a faith rooted in history compels an appropriate modesty in the claims we make as people of faith. It means giving up the desire for an indubitable faith, one that is impervious to doubts. The spirit of reason, science, and technology has fed this desire for rational certainty in one's faith, contributing to the modern inclination to summon rational arguments to bolster and vindicate the claims of faith. From the modernist viewpoint, postmodern theology would turn faith into fideism, a term that describes a "blind faith," or one that is lacking in rational support. On the other hand, postmodern theology can claim the insights of Christian existentialism, where Søren Kierkegaard (1813–1855), another precursor of postmodern theology, aptly characterizes faith as a leap—not a blind faith but a faith-commitment that bears significant risk, paradox, and uncertainty.

The conclusion I draw from a Christian perspective is that the shift in postmodernism from a focus on reason and universalism to a focus on faith and the particularities of history actually serves the church's theology. Revelation takes place in history, after all, a fact that has always been a stumbling block to modern thought. That is because modernism has polarized rational truth and historical truth, making the one universal and absolute and the other particular and contingent, the result of chance or happenstance. But the Christian gospel is rooted in historical narratives rather than a conceptual world beyond history. It invites one to an *encounter* with truth, something much more than a mental activity. Just how we should relate a history-based, revelation theology and a rational or natural theology has been an ongoing debate among Christian theologians, which we shall discuss in chapter 6.

From a modernist perspective, the rejection of universal truths would also appear to deny the reality of God, the source of universal truth. Postmodern theologians counter that they are simply recognizing human finitude. They take seriously the fact that we are historically situated and consequently limited in what we can claim to know when it comes to ultimate truths affirmed by religious faith. We do not have the big picture, which is necessary to grasping the whole truth. Westphal suggests that it may be appropriate for Christians to say that the truth-claims of their faith are *penultimate* rather than ultimate.[6] This would recognize that we ought

---

6. Westphal, ed., *Postmodern Philosophy and Christian Thought*, 3.

not claim that our theology provides an all-inclusive, unqualified final truth, but bears the marks of contingency that reflect the historical nature of human existence. Modernist theologians would call this relativism, while postmodern theologians would call it honesty, recognizing our limited, finite nature and the contextual character of our religious affirmations.

This view would find support in the words of the Apostle Paul, for whom divine truth to people of faith is "like the dim image in a mirror" (1 Cor 13:12). For Paul, not until the final consummation can we see and know the fullness of the truth that inspires our present journey. Recognizing this fact should temper our inclination to make absolute and exclusive claims about possessing the truth. It should also lead us to question the modernist view among theologians who assume that their beliefs about an ultimate truth necessitate the falsehood of any beliefs that differ from their own. This confidence, which defines the truth of God exhaustively in terms of correct beliefs, cultivates a dogmatic spirit that cannot accept the possibility of error or an inadequate grasp of the truth. It is no exaggeration to say that this kind of dogmatism has been a most tragic feature of the religious temperament.

The Pluralist World

The decisive impact of culture in the consideration of truth is a major part of postmodernism's recognition of pluralism. Christians with a modernist view of truth are likely to regard this culture-centric view as a covert form of relativism and a threat to the truth of the gospel. There are certainly those postmodern philosophers who espouse a relativist view, but this is not the only option. Theologians will conclude that our historical, culture-centered existence makes contextualists of all of us. They are not denying the truth of the gospel, but reject the notion that we have a Godlike view of it that erases our limited, contextual perspective. They argue that the fault lies with the modernist version of reason, which would lift us out of existence and place us on a pedestal that provides a universal view of the ultimate meaning of things. For many centuries this claim or assumption has marked that branch of philosophy called metaphysics, and perhaps the significance of postmodernism for theology is most dramatic at precisely this point.

If the Christian accepts the fact that philosophy is guilty of overreach when it engages in metaphysical reasoning about the big picture, it does not mean that faith in God is excluded or that there is no final truth. It *does* mean that the grounding of faith is not in what the rational intellect can arrive at or what it might seek to prove, but in the power of the gospel in addressing the larger issues of human existence (in Blaise Pascal's words, that which involves "reasons of the heart"). Our inability as Christians to reach agreement on a host of theological issues is a reminder that in matters of faith, reason is no guarantee of a conclusive answer.

A candid view of Christianity itself would have to acknowledge that pluralism is alive and well within its own tradition, where believers bring significant variety to the way in which that tradition is experienced, interpreted, and practiced. That fact is often perceived as an embarrassment, generating attempts to enforce a desired uniformity. On the other hand, finite efforts to understand and articulate the tradition can be seen as inevitable, making pluralism a fact of life. Rethinking theology today cannot avoid the impact of pluralism, which at best compels an open spirit in our relationships with those who do not share our convictions. It invites the recognition that we are all in the same boat, with no one capable of "pulling rank" on his neighbor. No one can claim a pipeline to the Truth that establishes his own faith and invalidates all the others.

In countering the accusation of relativism, postmodern theologians also point out that the historical origins of religious truths do not deny their universal implications. Being situated in a particular historical and cultural setting does not prevent religious insights of universal scope from being made. Kathryn Tanner makes this point:

> Theologians can proclaim truths with profound ramifications for the whole of human existence; that they do so from within a Christian cultural context simply means that the claims they make are shaped by that context and are put forward from a Christian point of view. Indeed, if, as an anthropologist would insist, assertions always show the influence of some cultural context or other .... [T]hat is the only way that universal claims are ever made.[7]

In summing up, the negative criticism evoked by postmodernism should not prevent us from celebrating its positive features, whether as a cultural expression or in its recontextualization espoused by postmodern theologians. I would cite the following:

---

7. Tanner, *Theories of Culture,* 69.

- Its critique of reason challenges the autonomous reason of modernism that has led to an uncritical exaltation of science and technology, defining life's meaning in terms of human dominance of nature and the material benefits it brings to a consumer society;
- The critique of reason also opens up the possibility of a broader appreciation of human experience, including the role of imagination as a defining trait of what it means to be human;
- The modernist dichotomy between reason and its universal truths and the realm of history with its relative truths is repudiated, giving space to the religious claim of truth centering in events of history;
- The recognition of the decisive role of culture in shaping human identity and the consequent affirmation of pluralism beckons us to greater appreciation of other cultures of the world, including their religions, rather than seeking to denigrate them by absolutizing the values of our own;
- The critique of reason enables a proper and fruitful understanding of Christian truth in terms of the faithful life (living "in Christ") rather than correct or orthodox doctrine;
- The critique of reason also challenges the dominance of theology in church relationships, which magnifies our differences and contributes substantially to the fragmented, denominational character of the church today;
- The critique of patriarchalism in our society and colonialism in the international sphere promises a more integrated society and world.

There is indeed a yes and a no in our response to postmodernism, but there is much to be gained in affirming the positive. The mixture of positive and negative features that the church encounters in every culture requires a discriminating response; a wholesale repudiation of a culture is never an option for the church's theology. Given human nature, there will always be openings in every culture where the gospel can be fruitfully proclaimed and interpreted. Those openings, I believe, are certainly present in our postmodern age.

Chapter Four

A Modest Proposal

It is not the intent of theology simply to set forth, amplify, refine, and defend a timelessly fixed orthodoxy or a systematic theology.... [T]he work of theology is never completed in some sort of once-and-for-all fashion. It is a living enterprise, a social practice of the church that will continue without end.

—John R. Franke[1]

What I wish to suggest is that another way, a way I would describe as the *kerygmatic, parabolic tradition,* a way which depends on metaphor, is not only found in Christian sources but is at the heart of human understanding. We will not relinquish our idolatry in religious language unless we are freed from the myth that in order for images to be true they must be literal. Nor will we find religious language relevant unless we are freed from the myth that in order for images to be meaningful they must be traditional.

—Sallie McFague[2]

What I am proposing in rethinking the church's theology is a theological stance that is willing to acknowledge its limitations. In this

---

1. Franke, *Manifold Witness,* 116–17.
2. McFague, *Metaphorical Theology,* 32.

respect it could be called a "modest" theology, and what is meant by this should become clear in succeeding chapters. I see the notion of limitations embedded in a variety of ways in postmodern thinking, and I believe it is a fundamentally healthy notion for the task of Christian theology. The most obvious example is the postmodern rejection of the modern era's claim to possessing transcendent truth that is objective, universal, and absolute. A modest theology recognizes the overreach—the hubris—involved in such a claim. In this chapter I will describe what I mean by a modest theology under six headings, briefly stated here and to be further developed in the chapters that follow. Each of the six subjects in one way or other involves recognition of our limitations in doing theology.

Thinking about God

A primary example of what I mean by our limitations relates to our thinking about God. There is of course a long history of human thinking about the divine, with great variety in the concepts being used. The view that has identified the God of Christian faith is called *theism* or *monotheism*, a view that finds its place within that branch of philosophy called metaphysics. Metaphysical reasoning, as we have noted, addresses ultimate questions of meaning about the universe and humanity's place within it. Another way we can put it is that metaphysics addresses what is ultimately real, a subject that traditionally leads to the question of God. Metaphysics has been a staple of modern philosophy and expresses a modernist confidence in the ability of reason to understand and master the ultimate questions raised by human existence. In contrast, I am advocating "epistemic modesty," or humility in what we claim to know about God.

We now live in a time marked by skepticism concerning metaphysical reasoning, a distrust of any claim to arrive at God through reasoning or rational inference. It is also a time when people of faith bring a heightened sense of the transcendent mystery of God, and for good reason. The universe that we have come to know places our planet as a tiny speck in a corner of a galaxy of billions of stars, and that galaxy is just one among billions of others. It is an absolutely mind-boggling universe, incredibly immense, instilling a profound appreciation of the mystery that surrounds the notion of God. It compels one to recognize that the concept of God simply eludes our capacity to think and comprehend.

A Modest Proposal

The idea that God is ineffable, beyond our ability to describe, actually has a long history in Christian theology. It is referred to as "negative theology" (*via negativa*), in contrast to positive theology in which attributes are freely ascribed to God. Negative theology maintains that our knowledge of God is gained through saying what God is *not* because we cannot say what God *is*. Driven by our reason to achieve understanding and reduce the mystery, the church's theology too easily leads Christians to make excessive claims about our knowledge of God.

These two realities of an ineffable, "wholly other" God and a finite, earthbound creature should have enormous consequences for the nature of our theological claims. Christians are used to saying that the biblical revelation enables us to talk about God with confidence (or even, as some would say, to think the very thoughts of God), but we fail to take seriously the caution of reformers and mystics that even in revelation, God remains hidden. This reality also prevents us, if we are honest, from claiming that we actually *possess* the ultimate truth about God for that implies our mastery of that which we possess. It becomes a claim to ownership that invites a spirit of hubris because it not only refuses to acknowledge our limitations but turns the mystery of God into an object of possession. When that happens, the sense of awe and mystery that belong to faith threatens to disappear. We do not worship the God we possess.

The Language of Theology

If God is beyond our capacity to express and language fails when we would refer to God, how should people of faith understand the language they use when they speak of God? Christian theology has recognized for many centuries that our language is not simply descriptive when we refer to God, as though God were an object in this world. However, what that means has been interpreted in different ways (a subject to be discussed further in chapter 5). One may conclude that our language concerning God is indirect, functioning as a "pointer" that cannot hope to fully express the truth to which it points. I am suggesting that people of faith who speak of God in personal terms are using figurative language, the language of metaphor, parable, and narrative. In doing this, we are using images rooted in our common life that would express the *meaning* of God for those who believe in him. It is the language of the Bible, which overflows with imagery wherever it refers to God.

Thus the purpose of theological language is to express the meaning of God by reference to familiar subjects from our everyday life. That is a suitable definition of metaphor, where a word or words used in one context are transferred to another, bringing new insight or perspective. A Shakespearean metaphor provides a familiar example: "My love is a red, red rose." (No she obviously isn't, but yes, she is!) In theology our words function in the same way, not literally describing the mysteries of faith, such as God or the incarnation, but indirectly or figuratively conveying what we are moved to say by those mysteries. In this context that is the best we can do, with the mind of faith recognizing that it is also enough.

Jesus himself is our prime example. As we know, when he spoke of God he spoke in parables, which we understand as extended metaphors. In this way he unveiled the meaning of God in this-worldly terms, as in Luke 15 where he likens God to a father whose love reaches out to claim the wayward child, or a shepherd who seeks a lost sheep, or a woman who searches for a lost coin. This is not description in the sense of exposing an empirical fact, but the language of metaphor that expresses an extraordinary personal truth by using ordinary language about ordinary events. It brings together the divine and the human by using images rather than abstract concepts to express the personal meaning of faith in God. Thus, Jesus' use of the metaphor "Father" has profoundly shaped—and indeed has made possible—the Christian's experience of God. Metaphor is the primary language of personal faith, and when recognized as figurative language it cannot be dismissed as naive anthropomorphism. It is an alternative language to that of metaphysics, which arrives at its own God as a rational concept.

Faith-Based Imagination

In recognizing metaphorical language as indispensable to God-talk, a modest theology also recognizes that metaphor is the language of imagination. It is risky for a theologian to speak of imagination because of its dual meanings that stand in opposition to each other. In our everyday world, an imaginary experience or an imaginary world can be a source of self-deception, waiting to be corrected by someone who has determined the facts of the matter. On the other hand there is the meaning I have in mind, where we recognize in the imagination our capacity for creativity and insight; the imaginative outlook is able to "see" or grasp what eludes the path of logical reasoning, or what lies beyond the reach of rational thought. When it comes to religious faith, the human intellect is in no position to give us the facts of the matter.

> Essentially it is the theological imagination which one must rely upon to communicate something of the mystery of God's reality. Without imagination, mystery remains obscurity; with imagination, mystery conveys something of the meaning of the absent and present God.[3]

In both philosophy and theology, following Aristotle and Thomas Aquinas, reason has been identified as the distinctive, defining characteristic of the human being, and as I have noted, that idea has prevailed throughout the modern period. The spirit of postmodernism is helping us to recognize that the imagination can just as well be seen as the uniquely human attribute. What it means to be created in the image of God must include the fact that we are creatures of imagination. Its scope is as wide as human experience: imagination enables us to see ourselves in others and relate to our neighbor in a spirit of empathy, perhaps its most important gift; it is the creative spark that paves the way for insight and fruitful knowledge in every discipline, from the humanities to the natural sciences; and when it comes to the divine Mystery, it is the imagination that enables people of faith to speak about God in personal terms. Thus imagination is the language of relationship. Where reason leads to God as an object, implying a measure of distance between the knower and the known, imagination *relates* the believer to God.

What we are saying is that the proper language of theology is not metaphysics from the realm of philosophy, but metaphorical language akin to the realm of art and poetry. This is to recognize that ultimate meaning, the subject matter of religious faith, requires imaginative discourse beyond the reach of empirical confirmation or rational proof. However, relating theology to art and poetry is not to equate theology with aesthetics. The subject of theology is God, while aesthetics expresses the human spirit in other realms of its creativity. The imagination is involved in both cases, but theology is rooted in a revelation that directs one to the mystery of God.

I like to speak of a "faith-based imagination," inspired by the life and ministry of Jesus Christ and enabling us to speak of the personal God whom Jesus addressed as "Father." It is not a concept of God that invites rational analysis, but an image of the imagination that places us in relationship to

---

3. Jones, *Christian Theology*, 39.

God as a loving parent. This is truly a gift of revelation that has the power to generate faith, and we could not receive it without our imaginative capacities. *Because of Jesus having lived among us, with his ministry and language concerning God, we are bold to imagine and speak of God in personal terms.* It is no exaggeration to say that the life and teaching of Jesus has transformed the image of God in the course of human history and throughout much of the world.

Unfortunately, believers invariably turn imaginative language into metaphysical statements which are then assumed to be rational and conclusive statements of reality. The God who is projected "up there" or "out there" is assumed to be an Ultimate Object of description, at least in a way analogous to our description of objects in this world. The result is an objectivized God in a heavenly realm. This way of understanding God not only denies the divine mystery but leads to all kinds of logical contradictions that threaten to trivialize the notion of God. The problem is compounded when believers are tempted to treat the God who is out there as readily available to solve our problems.[4] By recognizing the imaginative character of God-language—the language of meaning rather than a metaphysical description—we preserve the language of relationship without projecting God as "out there." That God too easily becomes an idol, an object of manipulation designed to satisfy whatever need we have at the moment.

Faith and Theology

A modest theology makes a critical distinction between faith and theology, or faith and beliefs. As a Lutheran theologian I admit that my tradition does not make it easy to recognize this distinction. We take our theology seriously, and while this has its positive features it also runs the risk of defining faith in terms of orthodox beliefs. That view has encouraged a doctrinal legalism with its hyper-orthodoxy among too many Lutherans, actually preventing full communion among Lutheran churches themselves. This has been an unfortunate offshoot of the Reformation, which created a situation in which the proliferation of churches with varying beliefs led to defining churches in terms of what was distinctive in their theology. This has

---

4. The German pastor-theologian Dietrich Bonhoeffer famously labeled this view of God as a *deus ex machina*, a God at our beck and call, a God at our disposal. Bonhoeffer, who was martyred by the Nazis at the close of World War II, can be seen as a transitional figure between the modern and postmodern eras.

encouraged the idea that Christianity is all about a body of beliefs rather than faith that generates a life of faithfulness to Jesus Christ. Purity of doctrine becomes the benchmark of Christian faith, with theology trumping faith rather than faith trumping theology. With faith at the center, theology becomes a servant of faith, among other things helping to keep faith intellectually and doctrinally responsible.

The word *faith* can be understood in several ways. It is commonly expressed in the Latin language as *assensus*, or belief in terms of giving assent to a theological or doctrinal statement; *fiducia*, or faith as trust in the living God; *fidelitas*, or faith as fidelity or faithfulness in one's walk with God; and *visio*, or faith as vision, seeing things as a whole.[5] While the substance of Christian faith is expressed in *fiducia* and *fidelitas* because they convey our relationship to God, there is a symbiotic or reciprocal relationship between faith and theological beliefs because each influences the other. This book on a modest theology is addressing faith primarily as *assensus* to the extent that it is dealing with *what* we believe as Christians and how we might interpret certain doctrines of the faith. While that is not the heart of what faith is about, it nonetheless has an indispensable role to play. Our theology does affect the character of our faith—among other things, the way we understand the Bible as the Word of God and the way we choose to express our faith in our relationships with those of other religious traditions.

While faith is thus closely bound to beliefs, I prefer to speak of *convictions* in this context rather than beliefs because it is a word that conveys more than just mental or intellectual assent. Convictions are beliefs that carry a "depth" dimension, that get to the core of one's faith. In the Christian context, these convictions would express the basic Trinitarian nature of our faith. But even here, our convictions are best served by a spirit of humility that acknowledges our poverty when it comes to the truths that we profess. In this postmodern age, doctrinal conflicts and the heresy trials that could occasionally accompany them appear quite passé, but this isn't simply to say that we can dismiss this dimension of faith. Convictional beliefs are intimately related to the life of faith. To deny, for example, the conviction that in Jesus the redemptive power of God is at work in the human family would compel a complete reorientation of the Christian's faith commitment and consequently her self-understanding as a child of God. But theology remains the church's response to the gospel message, not the gospel itself.

5. Borg, *The Heart of Christianity*, 28–37.

Theology of the Cross

A modest theology affirms a "theology of the cross," a phrase that is rooted in the Reformation where Martin Luther emphasized the cross of Christ as the definitive symbol of Christian faith, life, and theology. It was a revolutionary assertion because he contrasted it with a "theology of glory," which he identified with the church of his time. It was a powerful, triumphant church with a corresponding theology. The presence of God was visibly demonstrated by the church itself whose leader, the pope, was the "vicar of Christ." Salvation was dispensed by an infallible church, which endowed the sinner with an enabling grace that allowed him to cooperate in earning salvation. Faith was intimately bound to reason, the distinctive human capacity that was able to establish the very existence of God.

In contrast, Luther's theology of the cross was acutely aware of our human limitations. We do not in any way warrant divine grace but are totally dependent on God—"nothing in my hands I bring." The avenue to God is marked by a profound self-knowledge that we are sinners in need of forgiveness and renewal. This recognition of the fragmented character of our lives has led Reformation churches to use such radical terms as "rebirth" and "conversion" in depicting one's entry into faith. That life, in turn, offers no escape from uncertainty and doubt, leaving no alternative but to trust in the grace of God.

The theology of the cross brings a radical reorientation in our understanding of the divine. The omnipotent, all-powerful God becomes the God of the cross of Christ who suffers with us, whose power is made known in weakness, the power of a suffering, redemptive love. The life of faith is no heroic march of certainty nor a pass to security, but is renewed each day by our dependence on divine grace and mercy. This theology that testifies to the vulnerability and limitations of the believer was poignantly expressed by Luther on his death bed, where he uttered the words, "We are beggars; that is true." In Scripture it is Paul who most clearly expresses a theology of the cross in his desire "to know nothing among you except Jesus Christ and him crucified" (1 Cor 2:2). That was a revolutionary statement, both in the image of God it conveyed and in its implications for Christian faith.

A Modest Proposal

A More Hospitable Theology

A modest theology recognizes and welcomes the implications of the above statements for the church's relation to those of other religious traditions. For centuries, beginning with Emperor Constantine's conversion to Christianity in the fourth century, the church's place in western society was that of an imperial church. Its realm was Christendom, and it had no serious challengers to its religious hegemony. This situation continued well into the modern period, where Christians living in the West have been relatively secluded from contact with members of other world religions. This isolation and privileged position of the church has played its role in encouraging Christians to believe that salvation, generally understood as an eternal reward beyond the grave, is an exclusive gift of their faith. This belief presumably gives them the right, even the obligation as Christians, to render judgment of non-believers and to engage in missionary work to "save the lost."

In response to these interpretations and claims, a modest theology that is both true to the core message of the cross and closer to the spirit of Jesus will generate a more hospitable theology and consequently a more responsive engagement with the world. Our times demand a thoroughly ecumenical theology that stretches beyond the church to engage all religious traditions. If they are to bring a more authentic message, churches must abandon the imperial mentality that they often project, claiming superiority to other religions. This superiority is commonly asserted in the claim that only Christians will be "saved." The irony in this claim is that if the church is willing to relinquish the role of playing God, it will become a much more persuasive witness to the gospel of Jesus Christ. It then can become a genuine companion on the human journey with those who walk according to a different spiritual vision, addressing them as an equal rather than their superior.

It is not inappropriate to speak of a *healthy agnosticism* that belongs to the nature of faith, where we are willing to acknowledge that we do not have all the answers. That fact is certainly implied in the words of St. Paul: "We walk by faith, not by sight" (2 Cor 5:7). That is a fundamental truth for a modest theology, and it includes both objective and subjective dimensions. As people of faith we are challenged to recognize the objective fact that our knowledge is limited, but subjectively that reality challenges us to accept and even to embrace the sense of uncertainty and vulnerability that follows from that fact. Whether it is faith, hope, or love in human life, they are always fragile; no matter how saintly or devoted one may be, doubt, uncertainty, and a sense of one's own weakness are constant companions. *A modest theology would encourage us to think more deeply and honestly about the nature of faith as it is actually experienced and expressed in the lives of fallible human beings.*

I trust my discussion to this point has made it clear that Christian theology is an open-ended discipline. There are landmarks established along the way in the history of the church's theology, to which we return, but with the recognition that they need continuing review and re-understanding. The church's thinking about the gospel of Jesus Christ and the tradition that has evolved over the centuries is not a package dropped from heaven; it is the result of our encounter with the history, culture, and ethos that have formed us. It presents an ongoing task of interpreting the gospel, compelling a creative response. That response must always keep in mind its human, fallible character, which should give us second thoughts about any claims to holding an absolute and exclusive Truth.

The quest for certainty and closure are deeply embedded in the human psyche, especially when it comes to theological beliefs. Realistically, tempering that quest calls for a conversion of sorts, a profound change of mind about what it means for Christians to know the Truth. When beliefs regarding religious truth are believed to be decisive in determining one's destiny beyond the grave, the desire for certainty and the absence of doubt takes on particular intensity. We see this when it comes to interfaith relations, where certainty becomes an absolute imperative in the face of a perceived threat of an opposing belief. When our faith is centered on this life rather than the afterlife, a spirit of openness to the other is more likely achieved. Then *living* the Truth rather than *possessing* the Truth is the essential issue. The philosopher of science Michael Polanyi makes a point that Christians could profitably apply to their own beliefs: "[My] principal purpose . . . is to achieve a frame of mind in which I may hold firmly to what I believe to be true, even though I know that it might conceivably be false."[6]

What is distinctive about Christian faith in responding to this issue is that we are able to say, "In the midst of uncertainty and doubt there is one who speaks to me with authority, and that is Jesus." He does not completely remove the uncertainty embedded in the human condition, but he has persuaded believers to become followers, and in following a new life is born. His life and ministry, his death and resurrection, convey an authentic

---

6. Polanyi, *Personal Knowledge*, 214.

message that sets us on a path that is its own reward. We have not yet arrived at our journey's end, but the presence of Jesus—the Spirit of God with a human face—inspires our trust along the way.

Chapter Five

The Impossible Necessity
Thinking about God

God is the unknown God and precisely because He is unknown He bestows life and breath and all things. Therefore the power of God can be detected neither in the world of nature nor the souls of [humans]. It must not be confounded with any high exalted force known or knowable.... Being completely different it is the *krisis* [judgment] of all power, that by which all power is measured and by which it is pronounced to be both something and nothing, nothing and something.

—Karl Barth[1]

Made in the image of God, we grow in the image of the God we make for ourselves... We have, obviously, in our attempt to understand God as personal, configured the Godhead to be a person writ larger than ourselves. We have seen in that limited conception both the best and the worst, the most limitless and the most limited of ourselves. To make this partiality an absolute warps both God and us. I substitute my own limitations for the limitlessness of God.

—Joan Chittester, OSB[2]

---

1. Barth, *The Epistle to the Romans*, 36.
2. See Chittester, "God Become Infinitely Larger," 62–63.

The Impossible Necessity

I believe the title of this chapter conveys the sensibility of Christian faith in our time: a deep sense of the Mystery that is God, utterly beyond our comprehension and well beyond our capacity to think about. To state this reality is nothing new and certainly not revolutionary in light of Christian theology, but the breadth and depth of its meaning today is far more overwhelming than ever before. It was the ancient church father Augustine (354–430) who spoke of God as ineffable, beyond any words that we could possibly summon. All that we believers can really do with our words, he said, is to praise God. So it appears that we are faced with a contradiction, or at least a paradox, since the task of theology is to think and talk about God. It poses a predicament that has increasingly gained the attention of theologians in our time, bringing greater focus to the nature of theological language. Postmodern thought, with its understanding of language as a social construct, has contributed in bringing the subject to the center of attention, not only in philosophy and theology but in virtually all the academic disciplines. As we turn to the subject of God, it will be helpful to reflect further on the nature of the language we use when speaking of God.

Metaphysical Language and the God "Out There"

In the last chapter we noted the importance for theologians to emphasize that the language of theology concerning God is indirect, figurative language, or the language of metaphor. While Christian theology has recognized the symbolic character of God-language, throughout the modern era theology has remained wedded to philosophy in the form of metaphysics. The prefix *meta* is a Greek word that in this context signals a realm other than or beyond the physical world (*physis* being the Greek word for "nature"). Metaphysical language carries the assumption that we are making statements about an objective realm—not a fanciful, imaginary world but a noetic, intellectual realm that is accessible to our minds as rational creatures. This kind of thinking, though not unchallenged during the modern era, remains as a prominent legacy in the thinking of believers today.

The God of metaphysics, or theism in the context of Christian faith, has been traditionally described by a well-defined list of characteristics called attributes: God is eternal (self-existing), omnipotent, omniscient, omnipresent, and morally perfect. God also acts, so God must be personal and in some sense have a mind. The assumption is that if Christianity is true, then the God of theism must be valid and accurate; the belief requires that metaphysical conclusion, and that conclusion rationally validates the belief. This closely knit relationship of theology to philosophy has been dominant throughout most of the modern era.

I am one of many Christians who have concluded that metaphysical language has lost its viability in its references to God and no longer serves the purposes of Christian theology. Theism places God in a metaphysical realm "out there" where God is the Supreme Being, a kind of heavenly monarch; while the mystery of God is professed, the image succeeds in removing the mystery. The "out-thereness" of God has actually been an essential mark of the *reality* of God in the thinking of most of us, and yet it is precisely this God about whom it can be said, "Your God is too small."[3] *It would be helpful to Christians if they were able to recognize that we live in a post-theism age.* The God of metaphysics is no longer believable because it objectifies God as the Supreme Being—an entity in a class by itself—and as long as that kind of thinking persists there will be a religious and cultural crisis over the subject of God. One evidence of that crisis is the recent spate of books written by scientists and science-oriented writers declaring that God, rather than "out there," is "not there."

At least since the Death of God phenomenon of the 1960s the subject of God in western culture has been dominated by the question whether God exists. I believe a more accurate question is whether the God of metaphysics exists, or whether the God of traditional theism exists, or whether the word "exists" is even an appropriate term to apply to God. In other words, the issue is not about the reality of God so much as it is about the inadequacy of our thinking about God. This is obvious enough to theologians who observe the current science vs. religion debate. It is basically an issue of anti-theism rather than atheism, and Christians have something important to learn from this fact. The assumptions that govern both sides need to be revised if there is to be a fruitful dialogue on the subject of God. For Christians, there is no point in defending a God who is "too small."

The anti-theist nature of arguments of such writers as Richard Dawkins (*The God Delusion*) and Christopher Hitchens (*God Is Not Great*) is clear from the nature of the God they are attacking. As one writer puts

---

3. This phrase has become familiar through the book of the English clergyman J. B. Phillips, entitled *Your God Is Too Small: A Guide for Believers and Skeptics Alike*, published in 1961. Phillips is best known for his translation of the New Testament into a highly readable, contemporary style. His commitment to communicating the gospel in fresh and persuasive language is also apparent in *Your God Is Too Small*, where he takes issue with the church's traditional language in its doctrine of God.

it, they appear to subscribe "to what one might call the Yeti view of belief in God . . . the view that God is the sort of entity for which, like the Yeti, the Loch Ness monster, or the lost city of Atlantis, the evidence we have so far is radically ambiguous, not to say downright dubious . . . . One scarcely needs to point out even to first-year theology students what a travesty of Christian faith this is."[4] The whole debate has the character of fundamentalists on each side, submitting arguments that fail to capture the depth of the issues involved. The idea of the ineffability of God who is beyond the limits of cognition, or the nature of faith as something more than a proposition about the existence of a supreme entity out there, hardly enter the discussion.

In recent years Christian philosophers and theologians have settled on a more adequate concept than theism in their thinking about God, called *panentheism*. The emphasis in theism lies on the transcendence of God, a God who is out there, and thus when we speak of "acts of God" in history or nature it is difficult to avoid the idea that it involves some kind of intrusion, most likely a miraculous event. Panentheism unites the transcendence and immanence of God more effectively; as the word indicates, "all things are in God," but that is not understood in an exhaustive sense. That is, panentheism is not *pantheism*, which identifies God with the world. All three of these terms—theism, panentheism, and pantheism—are metaphysical concepts that function quite apart from biblical language and its image of God.

For the Christian, speaking of God and God's relation to the world is more appropriately expressed by the biblical word *spirit*. The "Spirit of God" is language that conveys both the mystery and the immanent reality of God. It captures the divine reality that the Apostle Paul refers to in Acts 17:28, where he quotes approvingly the words of a Greek poet: "In [God] we live and move and have our being." The language of spirit serves us well in deobjectifying God, coming as close as we can to speaking of the God who is "everywhere and nowhere" (a phrase which acknowledges that God is beyond our capacity to define). The church's traditional doctrine of the Holy Spirit accentuates the sanctifying power of God in the life of the believer, but spirit as the term is used in Scripture expresses God's presence in a much more comprehensive way—as in creation, the history of Israel, the life of Jesus, and the origin and ongoing life of the early church.

For Christians there are two words in the New Testament that are particularly definitive in our talk about God. They are used as predicate

---

4. Eagleton, *Reason, Faith, and Revolution*, 110–11.

adjectives: "God is love" (1 John 4:16), and "God is spirit" (John 4:24), where Jesus says, "God is spirit, and those who worship him must worship in spirit and truth." The particular gift of the word *spirit* is its ability to say what needs to be said concerning God's presence "in our midst" and in all of creation, what we refer to as the immanence of God. The mystery conveyed by spirit also expresses the transcendence of God, not in the sense of a distant deity but as a God who eludes our capacity to comprehend. Because of its ability to capture both the transcendence and immanence of God, spirit has been characterized as a "root metaphor for the sacred."[5]

In moving away from the theistic image of God, the twentieth-century theologian, Paul Tillich (1886–1965), has played a significant role. Tillich was a metaphysician at heart, referring to God in ontological terms or in the language of *being*, which serves as a word for reality. The most basic term that he proposes for God is "Being Itself," or ultimate reality. He also speaks of the "ground of being" and the "power of being," which he understands as symbolic expressions for being itself. This language has the merit of avoiding the spatial connotations of a God "out there" as the supreme existing being; rather, God is the *ground* of all that exists. Tillich's point is that existence is a concept that belongs to our world of space and time; it is properly applied to entities that live and die. To say "God exists," according to Tillich, is just as much an atheistic statement as to say "God does not exist." His shifting God-language from height to depth—evident especially in his sermons—has been helpful for many believers, providing a greater sense of ultimacy to one's thinking about God. But Tillich's supreme confidence in reason, or ontological thinking, raises its own problem.

We see this problem in Tillich's reference to "the God beyond God," beyond both the Supreme Being of metaphysics and the personal God of Christian faith. To think of God as personal means that we necessarily particularize or objectify God in our thinking, because the only way we can conceive of a personal God is to think of "him" as in some way *a person*. This personal God for Tillich is the symbol for the real God that is being itself. Thus Tillich gives a double meaning to the word "God": that One to whom we relate in our religious consciousness, and that One that is being itself.[6] This double meaning illustrates the difficulty that metaphysical reasoning poses for people of faith: there is the God of faith and there is the "real" God accessible to reason.

---

5. Borg, *The God We Never Knew*, 72.
6. Tillich, *Systematic Theology* vol. 1, 235–41.

Tillich disposes of the usual metaphysical God in his "thereness," but he is still captivated by metaphysical reasoning, claiming in the first volume of his *Systematic Theology* that reason's understanding of God as being itself is the only non-symbolic reference to God that we can make (a claim that was widely challenged among theologians—how can finite creatures say anything about God that is directly descriptive, or non-symbolic?). Though modifying his stance on this point, Tillich reflects a modernist perspective with his conviction that conceptual reasoning is the basis for our talk about God. Again, this confidence in reason is misplaced, denying the limits of our capacity to know the Mystery that is God. Christian faith finds a different anchor for our talk about God: Jesus himself, whose language is metaphorical and parabolic.

Evolution and Theology

The movement from theism, with its "monarch God" in the heavens, to Tillich's God who is the ground and power of being, to the appeal of panentheism and the increasing emphasis on the immanence of God, and to the use of spirit as a generic term for God, goes hand in hand with the growing impact of evolutionary thinking in our time. Since Darwin's epoch-making book, *On the Origin of Species* (1859), biological evolution has been perceived by many if not most Christians as a mortal threat to their faith and a menace to the morality of society. That opposition within the church has been surprisingly obstinate, making it difficult for theologians to recognize the promise that evolution holds for theology. It is important for theologians today to recognize the awesome process that is evolution, incorporating it with a dynamic use of the spirit metaphor.[7]

The growing acceptance of biological evolution within the church is a telling reminder of the powerful influence wielded by cultural change. Evolution is now an indispensable theory to understanding the world in which we live, and it has inspired fruitful ideas in many areas of human endeavor—including theology. The mechanistic, closed view of the world generated by the Newtonian paradigm is giving way to a more holistic, open view encouraged by the recognition of an evolving world. The whole notion of creation is immeasurably enriched and deepened by the process of evolution, a "continuing creation." While Newton's universe had no room

---

7. That task is now well underway. See, for example, Moltmann, *God in Creation*.

for God,[8] evolutionary theology identifies God as inherent to life in all of its many manifestations, leading to personal consciousness and the fullness of life in human personhood.

The Jesuit paleontologist and philosopher Teilhard de Chardin (1881–1955) was a pioneer in recognizing the significance of evolution not only for science but for the church and modern culture. His work is an unusual combination of scientific theory and metaphorical language, by which he interprets the material world using theological ideas and spiritual values of the Christian message. An ardent disciple of Teilhard today is Ilia Delio, a Franciscan Sister teaching at Georgetown University. Delio sees evolution as a critical factor in the movement from modernism to postmodernism, providing the church with a paradigm for understanding the meaning and purpose of the Christian life for our time: "In my view, evolution *is* the story, the meta-narrative of our age. It is not only a scientific explanation for physical reality; it is, rather, the overarching description of reality, the cosmological framework for all contemporary thought."[9]

The traditional cosmology in the church's theology portrays God in static terms and the universe as a static, once-for-all universe, finished and complete from its origin. It is a picture that is more at home in the medieval world than our own. Relating the Holy Spirit to creation, the Spirit becomes the dynamic, creative power of God that brings an open universe that has not yet reached its fulfillment. In the positive spirit of Teilhard, Delio sees love as the fundamental energy of evolution, generating new life and urging cosmic life toward greater unity. Whatever the metaphors one uses, the reality of evolution should play a significant role in the theology of the future church.

Metaphorical Language and the God of Imagination

To lift up the necessity of metaphorical language in theology actually runs against the grain of a long and well established tradition in the West. It goes back to the ancient Greek philosopher, Plato, and to theologians of

---

8. Newton was a devout man, and while his universe was a closed system he found a place for God in explaining the fixed positions of the stars that appeared to defy the force of gravity. With no explanation available at that time, Newton concluded that it was God who kept them in place, a conclusion still possible in the seventeenth century but hardly today.

9. Delio, *The Unbearable Wholeness of Being*, xvi.

the ancient church such as Augustine, who shared the conviction that truth and meaning can only be conveyed by conceptual thought, purified of all imaginative or pictorial content. Anything coming from the imagination is suspect, lacking in clarity and obscuring the truth.[10] This view has had its impact in the modern era, which has tended to regard metaphor as ornamental, identified with poetry and other artistic expressions in contrast to the conceptual, direct, and certain knowledge conveyed by reason.

The emerging consensus today is that the language of metaphor is inherent to the very nature of language. We are beginning to realize that the scientific temperament dominating the modern age has flattened the richness of language, giving the impression that all truth is to be equated with factuality, or what can be determined through empirical investigation. The renewed interest in metaphorical and parabolic language has been a godsend for theology, providing a fruitful alternative to metaphysical language in the midst of its waning viability.

A more careful view of metaphysical language concerning God leads one to conclude that it is actually dependent on metaphors. Speaking of God as "up there" or "out there" or down there" (ground of being) is to apply spatial language to God, obviously metaphorical expressions. One can say that the first two of these three spatial references ("up there" and "out there") are metaphors that have outgrown their usefulness ("dead metaphors"), while the third still has some life because the notion of depth or grounding of all things is more easily attuned to our thinking about the immanence of God. If we recognize these metaphysical statements to be metaphorical, then we are not trying to describe the indescribable. We avoid any suggestion that there is a Supreme Being whom we can actually describe—at least in an analogical or symbolic sense. That would be a metaphysical assumption.[11]

---

10. Gunton, *The Actuality of Atonement*, 16–17.

11. I should clarify my use of the word *analogy* because it can convey two different meanings, literary and metaphysical. Its literary use is metaphorical, where it likens God, for example, to a father, or to the wind. The Christian would understand those comparisons as both true and untrue, conveying a true meaning or insight but not to be understood as actually describing God. The metaphysical use of analogy goes back to Thomas Aquinas and his *analogia entis*, "analogy of being," where analogy assumes a continuity in being between God and humanity. This in turn justifies *describing* God as a father in an analogous sense. Because of that association I have refrained from using analogy as synonymous with metaphor, but others may appropriately use it that way when they define it in literary terms.

The question then becomes, on what basis can we think that metaphorical language is actually getting at the meaning of God? The answer of Christian faith is, "because of Jesus." We believe that in his own life and ministry he embodies the very meaning of God, a conviction that has led some theologians to speak of Jesus himself as an embodied parable.[12] His life, of course, did not take place in splendid isolation; he was a Jew, a son of his tradition, a peasant-carpenter, a wandering preacher and healer. But his message and deeds riveted the attention of his contemporaries, and his death-resurrection sealed his remarkable impact for all time. When he speaks of God his language is replete with metaphors, providing for the believer a manifold insight into the meaning of God. Because of Jesus we speak of God *as* a father, mother, provider, counselor, shepherd, rock, wind, and so on. While many of these words are embedded in the Old Testament tradition, Jesus brings them to life for Christian faith. His use of metaphor also drives home the open-ended character of his references to God; he is not intent on giving us an exclusive metaphysical definition, but rather brings numerous insights into the meaning of God with the variety of metaphors he uses.

The columns below may be helpful in comparing the language of reason and the language of imagination as related to Christian faith and theology:

Reason	**Imagination**
Concepts	Images
Abstraction	Concretization
Metaphysics	Metaphor, Narrative, Story
Natural theology	Revelation theology
God as idea	God as Spirit/Presence
God as ultimate being	God as "Father," etc.
God as explanatory principle	God in historical encounter
God of one's intellect	God of one's life
End goal: cognitive answers, removing the mystery	End goal: faith, living with mystery

Constructing two columns in this way can help us to see the contrasting nature of these two modes of thought, the one identified with philosophy and the other with theology. Where theology is treated as a sacred philosophy, it uses the language of reason and arrives at God as an exalted Idea. Where it is based in the personal, imaginative language of

---

12. Crossan, *In Parables*.

the Bible it conveys the God to whom we pray, the "Father of our Lord Jesus Christ." And yet, while this distinction is valid and important, there is room for conversation between the two approaches as we shall see in the next chapter. Nonetheless, it is imperative to recognize the distinction by acknowledging the faith-based, imaginative character of our personal language about God, and that we not confuse the Father image of God with the God of metaphysical reasoning. That God is typically a Supreme Object "out there," not to be confused with the God of faith, the Spirit who is present to us and in us.

When we fail to maintain the distinction between the two columns above, we end up treating the language of metaphor as metaphysical language, language that claims in some sense to be describing God. This is more than simply a confusion of categories. Feminist theologians have noted the profound social impact of the word *father* as applied to God, the result of treating a metaphor as a metaphysical truth. Conservative theologians have attempted to defend the sole use of father by insisting that it is the *name* for God and is thus irreplaceable and exclusive. On the other hand, as long as we recognize its metaphorical nature we acknowledge that "father" is one of many metaphors that can be used in reference to God. Then to use the word *mother*, for example, becomes a means of enriching the divine image by adding another metaphor rather than making a heretical statement. Feminist theologians have sensitized us to the idolatrous effects of absolutizing the image of father, where a metaphor becomes through common usage a dominant model for God, and then a name that would actually identify the male sex with divinity.[13]

This issue of calling God "Father" is complicated because there is a legitimate concern that Christians should not abandon the biblical language. This poses an irony, however, for biblical language refers to God with a multitude of metaphorical terms, overlooked or minimized in a patriarchal church. At a time when we are experiencing a crisis in our language about God, it is fortuitous that feminist theology enters the picture for it helps to drive home the metaphorical nature of God-language. The point is not to eliminate male language, but to challenge masculine assumptions that dominate the language and practices of the church. The church's task is to recognize and acknowledge its patriarchal heritage and to confront the evils it has imposed on women. Among measures that can be taken, the church's educational and liturgical materials need to emphasize the metaphorical

---

13. McFague, *Metaphorical Theology*, 145–52.

nature of God-language. This would justify and encourage the use of a variety of terms in reference to God, appropriate to different contexts in which the word is used—just as in the Bible.

The God of Metaphysics and the God of Faith

A further issue in regard to the God of metaphysics is whether this God of reason can be reconciled with the God of Christian faith, the God of the Bible. This question has been debated for many years, but the issues it raises have intensified in the postmodern era. Martin Heidegger, a significant figure in twentieth-century philosophy, refers to metaphysical reasoning in theology as "onto-theology," which arrives at an ontological God or a speculative God of being that is far removed from the biblical God. We noted this tension in Tillich's theology; the God of ontology is more like the God of Aristotle, a remote "First Cause." Heidegger sees this causal reasoning, characteristic of metaphysical proofs for the existence of God, as fitting quite well with the worldview of science and technology that is based on reasoning of cause and effect. But he notes that it is quite different from the language of faith. That faith, in light of knowing Jesus, is relational. It is more than a cognitive act in which we are essentially spectators considering the object of God. Faith is a state of existence marked by trust, dependence, and gratitude. The God of reason is not the God who is love (1 John 4:16), nor the God who summons us to faithful discipleship.[14]

With my critique of metaphysical, rational concepts that we see in the creeds and embedded in the church's theology, I am not saying that such language totally removed the personal God of Christian faith. Theology at its best has recognized the foreign character of its Greek-based, philosophical concepts and has sought to subordinate them to the personal language of Scripture, but with limited success. The assumption for most people is that rational concepts deliver a final, conclusive "description" of God and God's relation to the world, and for the laity those concepts are typically assumed to be literally true. For most Christians, I'm afraid, whether it is personal or conceptual language about God, the scourge of literalism results in a view that makes the notion of God a very questionable proposition. Ironically, the fundamentalist insistence on the literal truth of the biblical witness betrays its own kind of rationalism run amok. It establishes a mind-set that is incapable of appreciating the metaphorical nature of biblical language.

14. Heidegger, *The Piety of Thinking*, 10.

The Impossible Necessity

Given the personal, relational nature of Christian faith, it is no surprise that responsible theology has always carried a strong existential strain. It was powerfully present in the sixteenth-century Reformers, Martin Luther and John Calvin. Luther in particular was quite sensitive to the rational hunger for complete understanding, recognizing that it leads to reason's claim of sovereignty over the God of faith. In typically colorful (metaphorical!) language, he called reason "a whore" when it comes to matters of faith; in all other matters it does quite well.

Both Luther and Calvin acknowledge the unknown or "hidden" God, inaccessible to reason and hidden even in the act of revelation. This "wholly other" nature of God is a prominent theme in the thinking of the Danish existentialist, Søren Kierkegaard, who saw an inexcusable hubris in the rational system of his fellow Lutheran, the German philosopher, G. W. F. Hegel. He argued that Hegel's theoretical explanation of all of history—all of known reality, fitting into one comprehensive system of thought—was to assume the viewpoint of God himself. Thus Hegel has become a notable example of the hubris toward which reason impels us: total comprehension of all things in our quest for intellectual mastery, certainty, and security.

Kierkegaard makes his point with a quotation from the German philosopher and dramatist, Gotthold Lessing: "If God held in his right hand all truth, and in his left hand the lifelong pursuit of truth, mixed inevitably with error, and extended his hands for me to choose one or the other, in humility I would have to pick the left hand and say: 'Father, the pure truth belongs to you alone.'"[15]

This profound insight of Lessing is very difficult to acknowledge. A genuine faith, one that has the maturity to be self-critical, recognizes that the full truth belongs to God alone. A genuine faith is painfully aware that if we are certain about possessing the whole truth, we will exploit that fact as an expression of our own preferred status. Unfortunately that is a given, as history amply proves. Furthermore, when we claim the gospel truth as our possession we destroy its character as a gift, freely and graciously given. It is not something we have earned, attained, or achieved. It is, rather, the opening to a new life marked by repentance and renewal, where humility becomes an essential mark of authentic witness.

---

15. Kierkegaard, *Concluding Unscientific Postscript*, 97.

Chapter Six

On the Reality of God

> In essence, God's unlikeness to the finite world of matter and spirit is total. Hence human beings simply cannot understand God. No human concept, word, or image, all of which originate in experience of created reality, can circumscribe divine reality, nor can any human construct express with any measure of adequacy the mystery of God who is ineffable.
>
> —Elizabeth A. Johnson[1]

> God does not reveal himself except in act and in the Word, since these can in some way be grasped. The rest of what belongs to deity cannot be grasped or understood as it is.... Therefore wrappings (*involucra*) are necessary. It is unwholesome to dispute much concerning God before time and outside of time, because that is to desire to comprehend naked divinity, the naked divine essence .... But those who wish to reach God without such wrappings strive to climb heaven without ladders....
>
> —Martin Luther[2]

---

1. Johnson, *She Who Is*, 105.
2. Quoted in Baillie, *Our Knowledge of God*, 194–95.

On the Reality of God

I suspect that some readers may be questioning whether I am losing the reality of God with my reliance on imagination and metaphor. Am I paving the way for a disappearing God in this secular age? Is it an overreaction to metaphysics in theology and to the God of theism at which it has arrived? These concerns reflect a modernist outlook that is understandable in light of the rationalist heritage it has planted in our thinking. We tend to think that metaphysical statements are *explaining* what the truth is about God, without thinking about the assumptions that stand behind those explanations. They are simply taken at face value. A postmodern response challenges metaphysical thinking at just this point; it claims to know more than it actually does. As we have noted, postmodern thought also challenges the assumption that reason is the one reliable avenue to the ultimate Truth.

While I share this postmodern skepticism of rational attempts to reach God apart from the biblical revelation, we may still ask whether they bring something of significance to Christian faith. Are there perhaps *evidences* from reason, or from experience of the sacred, however weak and subject to dispute, that might give some measure of support to the notion of God? This is a question that draws a mixed response in postmodern thought, and it deserves further consideration.

Seeking God and Encountering God

Raising this question brings us to a critical issue in the history of theology. If human beings bear the image of God, as Christians believe, then it is quite natural to find among them a preoccupation with, and a search for, God. Human nature compels our asking questions about the meaning of human existence, questions that raise the possibility of a divine beginning of it all. There is also the fact of religious experience, leading to claims of a continuing sacred presence in the life of human beings. Thus, broadly speaking, we can discern two ways in which humans have responded to the possible reality of God: a *rational* response that would arrive at God from what we know and perceive about the world in which we live, and an *experiential* response based on the dynamics of the individual's inner life. Each addresses the mystery of God, or the question of an all-encompassing Truth that would bestow an ultimate meaning to human existence.

In the history of theology, either of these two ways of approaching the divine has been called "natural theology," or a theology based on the world of nature or the nature of the human being. I like to call it a "seeking theology" in which one seeks to arrive at God on the basis of what we know about our world and human experience. Natural theology stands in contrast to what Christians have called "revelation theology," which is based on particular historical events that are perceived as revelatory, or bringing God *to* us in some form of engagement. If we come to know God through historical events rather than through philosophical reflection, then we must speak of revelation. I would call this a "theology of encounter," where the movement is not from us to God but from God to us. Unlike a seeking theology, it is a faith-based theology, where the historical encounter generates faith that the Christian ascribes to the Spirit of God. In the Christian context, of course, these historical events center in the life and ministry of Jesus, his cross and resurrection.

How to understand the relation of natural to revelation theology has been a contentious issue during the twentieth century. On the one hand were those who saw the need of stressing the uniqueness and exclusivity of the revelation in Christ, with a correspondingly negative view of natural theology whose God is not the personal God of Christian faith. Karl Barth, the noted Swiss theologian, was a particularly prominent representative of this view; his theology created an exclusive either/or, in which natural theology was perceived as contradictory to a theology of revelation and a threat to an authentic Christian faith. On the opposing side were those who saw the need of establishing a point of connection between humanity and God, relating the Christian message to human nature and its quest for God. It is a debate, however, which should not conclude with an either/or decision.[3]

If there is substance to both sides of this argument, which I believe to be true, then one seeks a conclusion that does justice to the concern of each. Those who argue the exclusive truth of revelation theology are certainly right in maintaining that the God revealed in Christ as the Author of creation is hardly a datum of human reason or experience. Apart from faith, that God is more likely a *question* in the minds of thoughtful people rather

---

3. Undoubtedly the most dramatic event in this controversy occurred between two giants of the neo-orthodox movement, Karl Barth and Emil Brunner. Neo-orthodoxy, also called Theology of Crisis and Dialectical Theology, was dominant in Europe and North America during the first half of the twentieth century. Barth and Brunner were united in their repudiation of liberal Protestant theology, but could not agree on a common approach to natural theology. In response to a publication of Brunner that maintained a place for it, Barth published a refutation entitled, simply, *Nein! [No!]*. Many years passed before the two were able to reconcile.

On the Reality of God

than a conviction. On the other hand, to know the God of faith is testimony to one's having been *grasped* by the witness to that God and set on a path marked by trust in God. In other words, for the Christian to know the God of revelation is much more than head knowledge; it involves knowledge of the heart and a commitment to the God whom Jesus called "Father."

The God of natural theology is the God whom Luther, in the above quote, describes as impossible to reach—it's like trying to reach heaven "without ladders." We need "wrappings," such as the Word of God that *reveals* the God of creation, inspiring faith. As we've noted, imagination provides the matrix for this kind of response to divine revelation, as in the Christian's response to Jesus and the God he addresses as Father. The imagination responds to the notion of a personal, revealed God, leading some to conclude that the imagination can be understood as the "point of connection" between natural and revelation theology.[4]

This revealed God is proclaimed and transmitted from generation to generation by means of a community created by faith in that God. This is the distinctive shape of revealed religion, beginning with events that surround a charismatic individual and the consequent forming of a religious community with its sacred scriptures. In the course of history that religion becomes wedded to the cultures in which it has been planted, providing the substance or character of those cultures. Thus Christianity with its Jewish heritage has profoundly shaped the culture of the West, Islam has done the same in the Near East and Central Asia, and Buddhism in the Far East.

On the other hand, natural theology, building on human reason and experience, arrives at a God that is difficult to reconcile with the God of the Christian gospel. We saw this in the metaphysical reasoning of Paul Tillich where he arrived at "Being Itself." This God is the creation of the human intellect, an idea that has little to do with "the God of Abraham, Isaac, and Jacob." God is an idea that serves the purpose of providing a rational answer to the questions raised by human existence. And yet, the question of God in whatever form it takes can be seen as potential soil for planting the seed of the gospel. A good example from Scripture is Paul's encounter with philosophers at the Acropolis in Athens (Acts 17). Though his effort was resisted, he was right in relating a truth from their tradition to the gospel of Jesus Christ. When it comes to the reality of God, the language of the inquiring intellect may not be the language of the Bible, but it nevertheless

---

4. Green, *Imagining God*, 42–43.

can be its own witness to a universe that is not closed but open to the mystery of "Something More."

As we have seen, natural theology's assumption of a universal reason or universal human experience that gives rise to the notion of God is not well received by postmodern thought. It exemplifies foundational thinking, with its universal reason and universal truth. Thus it contradicts the postmodern thesis that our rational and experiential life reflects the dominant historical, cultural, and religious tradition in which we have been raised; no one's reason or soul is an empty tablet. We all bear the impact of a particular culture and the religion embedded in that culture, which has its effect on whatever form a natural theology might take. The skepticism about metaphysical reasoning and the rejection of "onto-theology" (ontological, or reason-based theology), as in Heidegger, also leads to a severe judgment of natural theology.

While I agree with the importance of making a clear distinction between natural and revelation theology, a seeking theology and a theology of encounter, there is another truth that postmodern thought does not sufficiently appreciate: contrary to secularism, the reasoning in natural theology expresses the fact that we human beings are religious creatures, seeking answers to questions that are ultimately religious. The human being looks for meaning and purpose in life, both in the daily routine and in the larger horizons of human existence. In this quest one finds connection between natural and revelation theology; to discount this connection for the sake of maintaining the uniqueness and truth of the Christian revelation results in isolating that revelation, removing it from conversation with those who are seeking answers to the deeper questions of life. But we need to spell out that connection a bit more.

The Universe and the Question, "Why?"

Turning to what I am calling the rational response in natural theology, the most ultimate question of reason one can imagine is, "Why is there something rather than nothing?" Or, as the cosmologist Stephen Hawking whimsically puts it, "Why does the universe go to all the bother of existing?" While asked with tongue in cheek, Hawking's question suggests an immensely intricate, mind-boggling universe that leaves us puzzled as to why or even how it got here. The "why" questions are the so-called "limit" questions raised by our reason, driving us to the limits of our knowledge.

On the Reality of God

The attempt to prove the existence of God is one way of answering these questions, but that route is hardly viable today. Nor is the atheist's response satisfactory to most people, where one concludes that the universe requires no further explanation; it simply *is,* and any questions it might pose concerning a "why" behind or beyond or within it are intrinsically unanswerable and not worth pursuing.

It is true that any rational answers we might arrive at in response to limit questions will be less than conclusive. Whether they lead to an ultimate meaning to the universe or to an ultimate meaninglessness, a nihilistic conclusion, they are never more than possible answers to the questions we raise. But the "why" question persists because of who we are as human beings. Our culture may be highly secularized, and the world of science and technology may provide answers to the human predicament that previous generations attributed to God, but the question of God does not go away. We may even find ourselves discussing whether God is "dead," but again, the question of God does not go away.

Given our situation as humans and on the basis of what we know about the universe, I believe it is possible to speak credibly of "evidences" that could point to a divine Mystery behind it all. While scientists tell us that we still do not know what lit the spark in launching the universe, it is clear that it proceeded according to a precise set of rules that have remained constant throughout the ages. We do not know if they pre-existed the universe, but they were there from the "Big Bang" beginning and govern to this day what can and cannot happen. These laws of physics that determine the subatomic realm are the DNA that has grown the particular universe in which we live. From physics and chemistry and finally to biology, each stage of the long history of the universe builds on the past, anticipating what is to come.

One of the great scientists of the twentieth century, Freeman Dyson, who cannot be identified as religious in any conventional sense, draws this conclusion:

> The more I examine the universe and study the details of its architecture, the more evidence I find that the universe in some sense must have known that we were coming. There are some striking examples in the laws of nuclear physics of numerical accidents that seem to conspire to make the universe habitable.[5]

---

5. Quoted in Giberson, "Cosmos from Nothing?," 22.

Some scientists are more explicit in the conclusions they draw from the awesome balance in the physical forces of the universe. They refer to an "anthropic principle" (from the Greek word *anthropos,* "human being") at work in all the coincidences that have led to the generation of human life. One can speak of a propensity in the evolutionary process that works toward increase in complexity, to consciousness, and finally self-consciousness in the human being.[6]

The whole universe works in a way that furthers order, not chaos. This fact is particularly astonishing in that scientists see, at the subatomic level, the appearance of contingency and randomness that does not create chaos but contributes to and maintains that order. In light of all this, one can understand the conclusion that we live in a world that can be intelligibly linked to faith in God the Creator. This is no final revelation to Christians; they fill in the blank of this unknown Creator God with the God they know in Jesus Christ and can take satisfaction in whatever support they perceive from this knowledge. It obviously leaves room for other views of God, saying nothing about the "character" of this God of creation.

My position here likely raises the subject of Intelligent Design (ID) in the minds of some readers. While I can appreciate the notion of design, it cannot be pressed too hard because of anomalies in nature that do not fit well with that idea. But more importantly, my problem with ID is that it poses as a respectable scientific theory of the universe, which it is not. When it speaks of design it implies a Designer, which would mean God in this context. However, we cannot introduce God as an explanatory factor in understanding the natural world without destroying the working assumptions of science. Advocates of ID maintain that a designed universe does not necessarily imply a Designer, but that is a hard sell. The religious believer will resonate with the idea of design, but to incorporate it in the scientific enterprise confuses the nature of both science and religion. The much more modest suggestion of Freeman Dyson is the most that a scientist can properly say, and I believe Christian faith should be content with that fact.

Science and Religion Converging?

Before leaving the subject of science and religion it is worth noting that the relation of these two spheres has taken a significant turn in the postmodern

---

6. Peacocke, *Theology for a Scientific Age,* 219–21.

era. Throughout the modern period that relation has been dominated by suspicion and hostility, so much so that their relation has been popularly characterized as "warfare." Part of that conflict has been due to overreach on both sides. Too many Christians have treated the Bible as a science textbook, and on that basis have disputed scientific conclusions that conflict with their version of "what the Bible says." On the other hand, too many scientists have exalted the empirical method as the sole avenue to establishing what is ultimately true or false. This latter view, referred to as "scientism," often expresses itself by arguing a materialistic, reductionist view of reality in which all of life, including human consciousness, is reduced to the interplay of atoms and molecules. That version of the microcosmic realm becomes the ultimate explanation for everything.

Beyond these extreme positions, there is the long-standing philosophical divide between the two realms, contributing to their estrangement. Science is rooted in the natural world and committed to the empirical study of matter, presumed to be the world of facts subject to direct observation and description. The philosophical expression of this view is materialism—reality is made up of matter in many different forms. On the other hand, religion lifts up the realm of the spirit in human life—God, soul, consciousness, faith—where one finds the essential realities of life in contrast to the material world. Throughout the modern age this dualism of matter and spirit has prevailed, creating an unbridgeable divide between the two realms of science and religion.

That divide, however, is not as convincing today as it was in the modern era. In physics, for example, the realm of subatomic particles defies observation and description, requiring creative imagination in the use of models that connect mathematical formulas to ordinary language. The scientist as well as the theologian is consigned to metaphorical language in describing what is indescribable. The distinction between matter and spirit has significantly blurred. With quantum physics, quarks, chaos theory, dark matter, and the Big Bang, we face a much more open universe, inspiring a sense of awe and a new appreciation of the mystery it poses at both the subatomic and cosmic level. Albert Einstein was one scientist who did not hesitate to acknowledge this fact, remarking that anyone who was a stranger to mystery is "as good as dead; his eyes are closed."

Philip Sheldrake, writing on spirituality, draws out the connection:

> [O]ur increasingly detailed knowledge of the fabric of nature—the myriad forms of life, the mesmerizing patterns of evolutionary

development, the dynamic processes that link everything together—provoke a spiritual attitude in many people irrespective of their views on religion. The main point is that deeply spiritual sensibilities and rigorous scientific enquiry are not incompatible despite some common misconceptions. Indeed, as the best scientists affirm, the more we learn the less we really *know* with definitive certainty.... At its deepest, science is itself literally awesome and inevitably provokes creative imagination.[7]

The point is also made that underlying the work of science is a belief that itself cannot be demonstrated by the methods of science. It operates as an assumption that is taken for granted but that can be seen as an article of faith, namely, that the universe is rational; it displays an order that makes scientific work possible and purposeful. Without this belief the whole project of science is hardly conceivable.[8]

The notion of a rational order to the universe, together with the imperative to know and master the natural world in order to serve the needs of humankind, is embedded in the biblical story of creation in Genesis and the Christian doctrine of creation. That doctrine stands behind the birth of science and its offspring, technology, which is a distinctively western phenomenon. While science and technology have contributed mightily in making life more livable and humane, they are by no means unadulterated gifts. Our postmodern age is recognizing that the human misuse of these gifts poses a major threat to the future of civilization. No doubt that recognition will become more prominent in coming decades, contributing to a growing apocalyptic consciousness in the face of climate change and its accompanying natural disasters.

The Inner Life and the Question, "Who?"

Turning from what I'm calling the rational response to the question of God, based on the nature of the universe in which we find ourselves, there is also the experiential response based on the human being's inner life. Here it can be awareness of our finitude, or other kinds of awareness typed as religious or moral experience. An example from Tillich's theology is his reference to "the awareness of something unconditional" in human life that evokes the

---

7. Sheldrake, *Spirituality*, 57–58.
8. Newbigin, *The Gospel in a Pluralist Society*, 20.

notion of God.⁹ Tillich emphasizes the quest for meaning that is prompted by human existence, where our finitude as mortal beings gives rise to the notion of infinity, or ultimate being. But for Tillich this sensibility is not definitive for Christian faith; it leaves questions in people's minds and hearts about the "Who" or meaning of God, and that is as far as natural theology can take us.

A notable example of natural theology among Christian theologians is the view of Friedrich Schleiermacher that human existence is marked by a sense of absolute dependence, a consciousness that invites the notion of God. In the Christian context it is at the root of our sense of grace and providence. He uses the word *Gefühl* that translates as "feeling," but he is not just referring to emotions. It is more of an existential response to human finitude and the contingencies of human existence, perhaps best characterized as a "creature consciousness." Schleiermacher brought the spirit of Romanticism to theology, focusing on human experience rather than reason and expressing a deep suspicion of speculative reason in theology, akin to the spirit of postmodernism. While sensitive to intimations of divinity embedded in finite existence, Schleiermacher held to the supreme importance of Jesus and a historical revelation, factors that influenced his understanding of the feeling of dependence.

Another prominent example of an experiential basis for speaking of God is the thesis of Rudolf Otto (1869–1937) in which he describes an overwhelming sense of the holy in human experience.[10] This is a mystical account of religious experience, in which the individual is overcome by an immediate sense of the numinous, or a divine power that Otto perceived to be "wholly other," utterly unique, and outside of the self. Unlike Schleiermacher, who regarded God as an inference to be drawn from the sense of absolute dependence, Otto sees God as immediately present in this numinous experience. He characterizes this encounter as twofold and inseparable, both a *Mysterium tremendum* and *Mysterium fascinans* (a terrifying and fascinating mystery).

The writings of mystics from a variety of religious traditions run along similar lines, including visions and other sacred encounters. Mystics usually stand at the margins of the religious community, regarded as less than orthodox if not heretical, but they offer a rich history that testifies to the variety of ways in which humans encounter the numinous. It is a realm

---

9. Tillich, *Theology of Culture*, 61–62.
10. Otto, *The Idea of the Holy*.

of human experience that can give rise to bizarre claims that strike one as strange if not absurd, but the literature of mysticism includes many penetrating insights into the nature of human existence as lived by those with an intense awareness of the presence of God.

Another notable argument from human experience is that of Immanuel Kant (1724–1804), one of history's great philosophers whose work contributed to the ending of the Enlightenment Age. In one significant respect Kant can be seen as an early precursor of postmodernism: his skepticism in regard to metaphysical claims was a body blow to the Enlightenment's confidence in reason. Rationalists of his time maintained that the mind is endowed with a clear idea of God, the soul, and other metaphysical concepts, but Kant argued that all of our thinking is based on sensory experience; our minds are tied to this world. Without that base, metaphysical reasoning concerning God leads inevitably to antinomies of thought that reason cannot resolve, where two conclusions, each of which can claim validity, stand in contradiction to each other ("God exists"/"God does not exist"). After this critique of "pure reason," however, Kant presented another route to God through what he called "practical reason," maintaining that our moral experience justifies belief in God. Our moral sense requires an ultimate justice in the human story that would be inconceivable without God.

These arguments will carry various degrees of weight for the Christian, but my conclusion is that natural theology is a realm of human experience that is important to Christian theology. One does not turn to these arguments as a conclusive reason to believe in God, but neither are they simply irrelevant to faith. They do require a discriminating response, however. Natural theology can distort the Christian revelation by entering into the thinking of Christians in ways that diminish or warp the full impact of the gospel with its message of sin and grace. The offense of the gospel embodied in the cross of Christ finds no expression in the God of reason, whose God functions as a metaphysical principle rather than the God of Jesus whose meaning is necessarily expressed in personal language.

Nonetheless, there is a message in natural theology that can be seen as a kind of helpful partner to Christian faith. The fact that the universe and our own planet demonstrate an astonishing order and purposefulness in sustaining life is significant to one's faith in God. The fact that human mystical experience gives rise to thoughts of an infinite Mystery or a divine Presence in the midst of human existence is not just interesting in itself, but a reminder that we are religious beings. The fact that we are moral creatures testifies to meaning and purpose in human life, indications of a higher calling that fits with our conviction that we are children of God. With all that said, however, the gospel itself is the Christian's most powerful invitation to faith; these other dimensions of life can make their contribution to that invitation.

God as a Human Projection

One of the more significant challenges to faith in God in the modern era has been the notion that God is actually no more than a human projection. Two influential figures are associated with this view: Ludwig Feuerbach (1804–1872) and Sigmund Freud (1856–1939). Feuerbach was a German philosopher and anthropologist who maintained that theology is not the study of God but of humanity. In other words, theology has no genuine subject matter of its own; it is simply a branch of anthropology. He understood theological beliefs to be unconscious wish-fulfillments aimed at removing the fears that plague humanity, the most intense and pervasive being the fear of death. This accounts for the particular appeal of Christianity, which promises an eternal life beyond the grave. God is the projection of our unconscious desires, a figure endowed with features of an idealized humanity. Two generations later Freud provided a psychological explanation for Feuerbach's ideas, maintaining that religion is a reversion to childhood and that God is a father figure, a source of security to allay feelings of helplessness and guilt. Religion is a childish response to the trials and tribulations of life, a delusory life-mode in contrast to the grown-up realism of atheism.

This is a serious and disturbing accusation that should serve as a stimulus to self-examination on the part of Christians. Several questions come to mind: What is the nature of my faith in God? What kind of difference does it make in my life? How does it affect my relations with others and to the larger society? The view of Feuerbach and Freud is that religion is self-serving, that we are insecure creatures who need a crutch, and God as the Supreme Being answers that need. It is true that a prominent feature of every faith, including Christianity, is the recognition of our mortality and the many vulnerabilities of mortal life. There is much that generates feelings of insecurity even in the healthiest and most self-sufficient mortal. One thinks of Jesus' words, "Come to me, all who labor and are heavy laden, and I will give you rest" (Matt 11:28).

But there is a point to be made here: Jesus is not addressing a *weakness* in human life, but a reality that calls for honesty and humility. Recognizing our frailties and vulnerabilities is a measure of our truthfulness, and how we respond to these challenges as believers depends on the maturity of our faith. The view of faith in Feuerbach and Freud serves their purposes as critics of faith. They picture it as a naïve, wish-centered response to life's tribulations, a picture of weakness and even a flaw of character. There are undoubtedly those believers who justify that judgment—we noted Dietrich Bonhoeffer's reference to a similar misuse of religious faith. But the Christian faith addresses so much more than our mortality and our needs. The question is what kind of God I believe in, or better expressed in the personal language of faith, "Who is the God in whom I trust?" The God who is pictured in the biblical revelation is both the God of "steadfast love" and the God who calls for obedience and justice, a concern for the welfare of the poor and oppressed. Faith constitutes a calling to be active on behalf of the vision of Jesus, the kingdom of God.

That is one response to the projectionist view of God; a second is based on the natural theology we've been discussing. The projectionist view treats God as a Supreme Being, a metaphysical view that in the minds of most people objectifies God as a being "out there." This supernatural, theistic view of God is assumed by Feuerbach and Freud. By the nineteenth century that God was becoming increasingly easy to question and reject. Today, as we seek to fashion our thinking about God in a post-theism age, it is helpful to recognize the deeply rooted character of our awareness of the divine. Whether we speak of it in the language of Tillich, Schleiermacher, Otto, Kant, or some other thinker, the human response to God is something far more than believing in a God out there. Faith ushers in a sense of mystery and awe, meaning and purpose, relationships and vocation. It is this depth dimension that the projectionist thesis fails to recognize and address.

Most important for the Christian in responding to this critique is the faith generated by the story of Jesus, which has become the point of orientation for understanding oneself and the world in which one lives. One can understand the projectionists' failure to grasp the meaning of this faith as a life-orienting experience, for they do not share this faith. Another way we can put it is that faith is more than believing information about God. Faith is a process of growth in which knowing God as revealed in Jesus opens up new insights about oneself as a child of God and the fact that life is a calling. Jesus creates a new setting for self-understanding, putting the believer in relationship with a personal God. This reorientation is what we mean in saying that to know God is to know ("re-know") oneself. Because of these realities the Christian will regard the projection thesis as missing the mark, having little to do with genuine faith. But at the same time, given our lack of faith and the ways in which we misuse it, Feuerbach and Freud can well be an incentive for self-examination: are they speaking to me?

The Triune God

From its beginning, Christianity has been identified as a monotheistic religion. Born as it was within the Hebrew tradition with its strong conviction that God is One, the monotheism of Christianity was well established. But at the same time, with Jesus and his resurrection, it received a distinctively Christian modification: God is triune, three-in-one and one-in-three. Monotheism was affirmed, but now it was the unity of God that particularly needed to be recognized. From early on, the New Testament references to God reflect a triune or Trinitarian flavor. This is particularly evident in the writings of the Apostle Paul and those followers who wrote in his name, most often referring to God in binitarian terms (Father and Son), but also in Trinitarian terms (for example, Rom 5:1–5, 8:1–11, 15:30; 1 Cor 2:2–5; 2 Cor 1:21–22, 13:13). This Trinitarian direction of the early church's theology was driven by its conviction concerning Jesus: he is truly Emmanuel, God with us, and the Spirit he promised as his continuing presence became a creative power that gave birth to a community of faith. The church's understanding of God was now indelibly threefold, but always the one God.

A perennial issue in understanding the Trinitarian dogma[11] is whether it is language that conveys insight into the "inner life" of God, or what we call the "immanent Trinity." Can we in any way *describe* the relations between the Father, Son, and Spirit? In the context of our discussion here, are we capable of giving a metaphysical description of the relationships between the persons of the Trinity? From my rethinking of the church's theology, the answer would have to be negative. We want to speak of God in the language of Jesus: God is "Father" and God is "Spirit," and with the

---

11. The word *dogma* has a negative ring today and in fact is not generally part of the Protestant vocabulary. In the Roman Catholic tradition it carries a strong legal meaning, dogma being those basic teachings that church law commands must be believed. I use the term here because of its long history and also to signal the fundamental importance of the Trinity teaching for Christian faith and theology.

witness of the New Testament we also recognize that without Jesus we could not do that. The Trinitarian teaching would tell us that Jesus is *really* a genuine revelation of God, an authentic reflection of what God means to us, the very Word of God. Therefore, Jesus is inextricably united with God the Father and Spirit in the Christian confession.

The Gospel of John is one principal source for Trinitarian teaching. In that Gospel Jesus speaks of his relation to the Father, which is John's way of expressing the unity of Jesus with God and the authenticity of the revelation we see in him. As we will note in chapter 8, we see exalted metaphorical language in the Pauline letters concerning Jesus, which again confirms the authentic, decisive character of the fact that "God was in Christ." But to go beyond this New Testament confession, delving into the inner relations of the Trinity, is to create a metaphysical God that entices our rational nature to encapsulate and understand. The cost for theology is considerable, for it transforms Mystery into a metaphysical God of our own making. That God inevitably becomes a parochial God, one that is "too small."

What does this mean for the dogma of the Holy Trinity? *It should be understood as the church's theological response to the gospel*, an intellectual and imaginative construction whose purpose is primarily defensive, fending off the views about God that the church perceived as heretical when the dogma was hammered out. We see this clearly in the language of the Nicene Creed, the church's Trinitarian statement, which was adopted in 381 CE at the Council of Constantinople. Its language is dictated by the heresies it is designed to refute, giving it a decidedly fourth-century character. This is what makes the Creed difficult to recite today; its words and the concepts they convey are quite strange to twenty-first-century ears, but that language has been sanctified within the church's tradition.

A good example of this problem is the Creed's statement that Jesus is "eternally begotten of the Father." The language of Father and Son was regarded as a description to be understood in our earthly terms, which means that Jesus was "begotten," or born, while in eternity. These words were prompted by the position of Arius (256–336), a presbyter of the church in Alexandria, who maintained that if Jesus was the *Son* there must have been a time "when he was not." The orthodox party disagreed, placing the birth "before all worlds" as a way of refuting Arius. Given the alternative position of Arius (he wanted to incorporate Jesus into a dubious mythological framework of the time) they made the right decision, but their language was clearly dictated by the historical situation they were facing. Today that language is more of an obstacle than an aid for confessing Christians. There is not only the problem of understanding the concepts of an ancient dogma, but of mistakenly thinking that its language actually describes the divine nature.

Theologian Luke Timothy Johnson addresses this same issue but makes his point with a different vocabulary. Acknowledging that "all properly religious language claims more than it can demonstrate, define, or even understand," he regards God-language as mythic rather than historical or scientific. Myth finds its natural expression in narrative, which is what we find in the Creed concerning Jesus. His narrative begins with his pre-existence, coming down from heaven to earth by means of the Virgin Birth, and ending with the cross, resurrection, and his ascent back to heaven. With the beginning and end of this narrative—his pre-existence and his ascension—we are using mythic language that states the *meaning* of Jesus by means of an extended narrative. We are not literally describing events that took place at the beginning and end of his life.[12]

What the Trinitarian dogma does is to capture the threefold Christian confession and experience of God as Father, Son, and Spirit, or Creator, Redeemer, and life-giving Presence. The critical factor in this Trinitarian view is, of course, the historical figure of Jesus; to affirm that God really comes to us in the person of Jesus, the church was led to *identify* Jesus with God, using language from the Greek philosophical tradition to say that Jesus was of the *same substance (homoousios)* as the Father. This metaphysical language seemed to be the appropriate way—indeed, the necessary way in their minds—of making this point, and we can respect that fact. We should also respect the fact that this kind of language is no longer our own, both in terms of the concepts that are used and the assumption they exhibit, namely, that reason is able to demonstrate the nature of God by building upon the scriptural witness and going well beyond it.

The notion of a "social Trinity" has been popular in recent years, where the relations of Father, Son, and Spirit are lifted up as an example for the Christian community. Luke Timothy Johnson, for example, sees practical benefits in imagining God in communitarian terms, encouraging mutuality and a spirit of love.[13] The word *imagining* signals the proper understanding of this point, but speaking of the persons of the Trinity as separate conscious entities who engage in social relationships risks serious

---

12. Johnson, *The Creed*, 54–55.
13. Ibid., 252.

misunderstanding. The meaning of the Latin word *persona* in the ancient world was not the same as "person" in English. The term was used in the context of Greek and Roman theatre to designate the mask used by an actor in the act of impersonation; it was a "face," signifying a role being played. This fact should discourage any attempt to "describe" the inner life of the Trinity, which is not there to be described.

Unfortunately, the setting of the three persons as conscious entities, side by side, has justified the charge of tritheism, or three gods. We are given the impression that the mystery of the Trinity is essentially a mathematical problem, where we are challenged to believe that in this case 1+1+1=1, not 3. Neo-orthodox theologian Emil Brunner points out that the Trinity is not and was never intended to be a mathematical puzzle:

> Through the Spirit we see the Son as the Son of the Father, and through the Son we see the Father as the Father of the Son, and as our Father. The three Names do not stand alongside of one another but after one another . . . It was never the intention of the original witnesses to Christ in the New Testament to set before us an intellectual problem—that of the Three Divine Persons—and then to tell us silently to worship *this* mystery of the "Three-in-One." There is no trace of such an idea in the New Testament. It is a mystery which the Church places before the faithful in her theology, by which she hampers and hinders their faith . . . .[14]

From the beginning theologians have used metaphorical language to enrich the church's Trinitarian teaching. A particularly apt metaphor was used by the church father Irenaeus (130–202), who spoke of the Son and Spirit as "the hands of God" at work in the world, effecting the will and purpose of the Father. Contemporary theologians continue to bring nuance and insight to Trinitarian thinking, as in a recent work of Paul Santmire in which the three persons are integrated with the metaphors "Giver, Gift, and Giving." In these terms he captures the gospel message of divine love and grace, understanding the Spirit of God in cosmic terms as the agent of life throughout the universe.[15] The Trinity dogma serves its purpose when its language is rightly understood, and when it helps to keep us faithful to the God portrayed in the New Testament, just as it was intended to do from its beginning.

---

14. Brunner, *The Christian Doctrine of God* vol. 1, 223, 226.
15. Santmire, *Before Nature*, 102.

Chapter Seven

The Historical Jesus

> Two worlds are colliding; amazement prevails . . . Jesus declares an inversion of the world's order, whereby the first shall be last and the last first, the meek shall inherit the earth, the hungry and thirsty shall be satisfied, and the poor in spirit shall possess the Kingdom of Heaven. This Kingdom is the hope and pain of Christianity; it is attained against the grain, through the denial of instinctive and social wisdom and through faith in the unseen.
>
> —John Updike[1]

"The glory of God is a human being fully alive," wrote Irenaeus of Lyons some two thousand years ago. One of the reasons I remain a Christian-in-progress is the peculiar Christian insistence that God is revealed in humankind—not just in human form but also in human being. This insistence shows up most often in the Christian claim that God was made known in Jesus. In Jesus, Christians believe, everyone gets a good look at what it means to be both fully human and fully divine—not half and half, as if he walked around with a dotted line down his middle, but fully both, all the time. His full humanity was on full display as he taught, healed, fed, and freed people, just as it was when he honored the poor, defied the powerful, and

---

1. Updike, "The Gospel according to St. Matthew," 8–9.

Christian Faith in Our Time

turned the institutional tables along with his own cheek.

—Barbara Brown Taylor[2]

In the previous two chapters I have contended that for Christians, what we can say about God is dependent upon the life of Jesus. This poses some formidable problems, not least whether we can believably say that a figure living over 2,000 years ago, a peasant carpenter and wandering rabbi from a remote part of the civilized world, can bear the weight of such a claim. Are we really to say that the God of the universe is decisively revealed in this little corner of the world? The answer would likely be negative were it not for the remarkable events that followed the execution of Jesus. His followers encountered him in the days following his death, an experience that inspired their cry, "He lives!" That Easter experience created a Pentecost community that ascribed their new life to the Spirit of God; they now knew Jesus in a fresh and powerful way. It had become clear to them that Jesus was indeed the Christ (from *christos*, a title meaning "the chosen one of God"), whose life was the very embodiment of the gospel he proclaimed, the "good news."

From a modernist point of view, however, there would be another reason to question whether any claim to a final, universal truth could originate from, or be based upon, historical events. As we noted in chapter 3, the rationalistic thought of modernism creates a divide between the realm of reason with its universal truths, and the realm of history with its particular, changing truths bound by time and space. In the mind of the Enlightenment thinker Gotthold Lessing (1729–1781), this divide formed a "great ditch" that defied every attempt on the part of historical, "revealed" religions to overcome with their own claims to universal truth.

This ditch has been challenged by postmodern thought, which reminds us that all of our truths are historical truths, shaped and colored by the historical, cultural roots that gave them birth. This historical insight marks my rethinking of theology, but as we have noted, it need not result in historical relativism. Recognizing our common humanity enables the communication of truths and insights that transcend cultural bounds, at the same time acknowledging the limitations imposed by our finitude and historical context. But history as the bearer of the Christian message does

---

2. Taylor, *An Altar in the World*, 118.

pose its particular issues, and we need to address them in light of the claims we are making about Jesus.

The Jesus of History

How much do we actually know about Jesus of Nazareth? How reliable are the accounts we have about his life? Does historical research provide enough information about him to satisfy the needs of faith? These questions pose issues that biblical scholars and theologians have wrestled with for centuries, referred to as "the quest for the historical Jesus." Some would say it is not a consequential issue, claiming that the church's message does not ultimately depend on historical events. Others would say it is not an issue that can be resolved, so the only alternative is to put it aside. But a theology that centers on Jesus as its source for speaking of God and "knowing" God would have to disagree for at least two reasons. One is the necessity of anchoring the historical basis of the Christian revelation; given the claims we have made about Jesus, he must have been a genuine historical figure who lived in first century Palestine. And secondly, it is necessary that we can determine to a reasonable degree that the person of Jesus as we know him "fits" with the claims that are being made of him. He could hardly have been a rogue or a deceitful person, or even one who was not involved in the common life of his people.

The historical scholarship devoted to Jesus over the past several centuries is truly extraordinary. It has greatly enhanced our knowledge and understanding of the religious, social, and political environment in which he lived, which in turn has brought new insights to his life and message. While it is unlikely that any historical figure has been subjected to as much scrutiny as Jesus, it is also true that historians have not had much to work with. We have nothing written by Jesus himself, and those accounts of his life that we have pose some challenging problems. The principal sources are the four Gospels of the New Testament—Matthew, Mark, Luke, and John—whose authors were his followers and far removed from contemporary standards of historical scholarship. The Gospels cannot be regarded as histories or biographies in the modern sense; they are often referred to as portraits rather than photographs, or sketches rather than detailed drawings. The Gospel writers have also been likened to four viewers at an art gallery, each bringing a particular angle to a great work of art. It is clear, too, that the particular audience each writer has had in mind gives a definite character to the Jesus they present. What this means in regard to the actual historical value or accuracy of the Gospels is a question that will never receive a uniform answer.

When it comes to non-biblical references to Jesus from the first century, one source often cited is Flavius Josephus (67–c. 100 CE), a Jewish aristocrat and military commander who wrote his *Antiquities* around 90 CE. His work is a valuable source of information concerning the Jewish world of Jesus' time. In a number of sentences about Jesus he refers to him as "a wise man" who was condemned to the cross by Pilate but whose followers have continued on to his own day. There are a few sentences in this record that refer to Jesus as the messiah and mention his resurrection, which scholars believe have been inserted by a later Christian scribe. There are also some rabbinical sources concerning Jesus, claiming that he "practiced sorcery" and that his execution was justified. These accounts, though hostile to Jesus, have historical value in proving that Jesus was a known figure whose message incurred the wrath of the religious establishment.[3]

Several Roman writers make passing reference to Jesus, including the historian Tacitus and biographer Suetonius in connection with the burning of Rome, which Emperor Nero had blamed on the Christian community. There are also several Gospels that have been found, bearing biblical names as their authors, but none maintain the authentic character of the four canonical Gospels. For example, stories of bizarre supernatural occurrences in Jesus' life are common, and he is typically portrayed as a divine figure appearing in human form, a view rejected by the church as a denial of his humanity. The most useful among them has been the Gospel of Thomas, which consists of many sayings of Jesus that are found in the New Testament, but very little narrative.

A critical issue for scholars is that the Gospels were written in light of Jesus' crucifixion and resurrection; those events receive by far the most extensive accounting because they are at the center of the Gospels' proclamation concerning Jesus as the Christ, the Son of God. To what extent has that fact colored their presentation of Jesus? Is this the "real Jesus" or a Jesus fashioned to suit the message about him? It is reasonable to assume that in the minds of the Gospel writers, the Jesus they were presenting was indeed the real Jesus; it is not likely that they were all engaging in some sort of conspiracy to deceive their readers. But the issue raised by scholars is obviously legitimate and deserves our attention.

3. Filson, *A New Testament History*, 67–70.

The Historical Jesus

It is helpful to see the Gospels as part of a developing tradition, consisting on the one hand of history as it was remembered by those who had been close to Jesus, and on the other hand history as it was being interpreted by the Christian community in light of the crucifixion and resurrection. The Gospels are a mixture of both, challenging the reader to discern where events and sayings of Jesus are history remembered and where they are history interpreted in light of faith. The latter convey a more overt expression of the meaning of Jesus, not just a recital of what happened. This is not to say that history remembered is true and the interpretive, metaphorical picture is false, but recognizing the distinction will contribute to a more accurate picture of the Jesus of history.

A good example of the development of the tradition can be seen in the difference between the Gospels of Matthew, Mark, and Luke (called the "Synoptic" Gospels because they tend to see things the same way), and the Gospel of John. The Synoptics were composed in the 70's CE, while scholars date John about twenty years later. What strikes the reader about John's gospel are the explicit statements that Jesus makes about himself and his relation to God the Father. In the familiar "I am" statements, he calls himself "the way, the truth, and the life" (John 14:6), the "bread of life" (John 6:35), "the light of the world" (John 8:12), and so forth. Still more explicit concerning his personal identity is the statement, "Believe me that I am in the Father and the Father in me" (John 14:11). These statements are commonly understood as conclusions arrived at by the post-Easter Christian community, which are projected back to the pre-Easter Jesus. Since the purpose of the Gospel was to proclaim the meaning of Jesus, ascribing these statements to him would not be regarded as inappropriate.

These statements in John are notably absent in the Synoptic Gospels. There the question of Jesus' identity typically focuses on whether he is the messiah, and Jesus himself seems to refrain from talking about who he is. For example, when the disciples of John the Baptist inquired about his identity, Jesus responded by pointing to his healing ministry and the good news he was bringing to the poor (Matt 11:2–6). In Mark 8:27–30, Jesus asks his disciples, "Who do you say that I am?" and Peter exclaims, "You are the Messiah." Surprisingly, Jesus neither agrees nor disagrees with Peter, but tells him to say nothing about it. Characteristics of this kind in the Synoptic Gospels contribute to the belief that they carry more historical veracity than does the Gospel of John. On the basis of the Synoptic Gospels alone it has been debated whether Jesus regarded himself as the messiah.

I personally believe that he saw himself carrying out a divine destiny such as that of the messiah, but unlike the Johannine Jesus he was appropriately discreet about claiming the historic title for himself. There were likely other reasons, too, for his reticence, such as the political atmosphere that was becoming more intense in the latter days of his ministry. One unusual feature of Jesus' ministry that would indicate a messianic consciousness was the fact that he would occasionally pronounce forgiveness to people who had come to him (Matt 9:2, Luke 5:20, 7:48).

Of course, this contrasting of the Synoptics with John does not mean that there is no theological interpretation in the Synoptics, but it is more modest in the metaphors that are used. The Gospel of Mark is the earliest of the four, and most scholars regard it as closest to "history remembered." Here and there Matthew, who clearly has used the Gospel of Mark as one of his sources, will at times expand theologically on what Mark reports. For example, in quoting Mark's account of Peter's confession, Matthew elaborates to make it a more explicit christological statement: "You are the Messiah, the Son of the living God." He then concludes the exchange with words from Jesus that would confirm the truth of what Peter has said: "Blessed are you, Simon son of Jonah, for flesh and blood has not revealed this to you, but my Father in heaven" (Matt 16:16–17).

While recognizing the challenges posed by the quest for the actual Jesus, it is fair to say that neither the question of his historical existence nor the appropriateness of what we know of his life in light of the claims made of him are matters of significant dispute among biblical scholars. There is good reason to see Jesus as a most remarkable, prophetic personality, one who "spoke with authority," inspired wonder, and attracted followers. Provocative claims will always be made about him, including those that are motivated by the desire to undermine the Christian message. They come and go because of lack of evidence. Given the nature of the case, Christians are content to believe that the Gospel portraits are as close to a picture of Jesus that we will ever have, a conclusion that I believe is justified. It leaves the issue of historical evidence open, as it must be, but what we know inspires confidence in the veracity of the gospel witness.

The Message of Jesus

Though the Gospels were written from four to six decades following the life of Jesus, the writers did have other sources at hand, including what scholars believe was the record of an oral tradition that contained his sayings (it is referred to as "Q," for the German word *Quelle*, meaning "source"). There is broad consensus among biblical scholars that the outlines of his message can be discerned with reasonable confidence. The central, framing message of Jesus' ministry was the kingdom of God that he was announcing as an imminent reality. Given the general absence of kings these days, the Greek word for "kingdom" could be more aptly translated as the "reign" or "rule" of God, or even the "presence" of God. The meaning traditionally stressed is that of a spiritual kingdom, or the presence of God in our individual and communal lives: "the kingdom of God is in the midst of [or within] you" (Luke 17:21).

More recent studies have brought out a political and even revolutionary character to what Jesus was saying, recognizing that his message was clearly antagonizing the religious and political establishment. Among significant parties at that time, the Sadducees and Herodians were on one side, intent on working with and profiting from the Roman presence, and the Pharisees and Zealots were on the opposite side, intent on undermining Roman rule in whatever way they could. Attempts have been made to identify Jesus as a member or follower of the Zealots, but they have not been convincing.[4] He may well have attracted followers who harbored expectations or at least hopes that he would lead a patriotic uprising against the Romans, and some have surmised that his failure to do so could account for a disillusioned Judas Iscariot who was led to betray him. I believe Jesus is most convincingly understood as acting in the tradition of the Old Testament prophets, bringing a critical and perceptive voice to the public arena, holding accountable those who wielded religious and political power, and summoning his people to spiritual and religious renewal.

---

4. A recent addition to books arguing that Jesus was a Zealot is Reza Aslan, *Zealot: The Life and Times of Jesus of Nazareth*. Aslan is a journalist by profession, but he has read extensively in the biblical literature. Of particular interest is the fact that he is a Muslim, which brings a distinctive perspective to his subject. I am aware from interfaith conversations that a common assumption among Muslims is that Jesus would certainly have led a guerrilla insurgency—acting like a Zealot—were it not for the dominant presence of the Roman military. This is a natural assumption for Muslims to make. Muhammad himself was both a spiritual leader and a military commander, and the golden period of Islamic expansion during the centuries following Muhammad's death was accomplished through military campaigns. The fact that the moral teachings of Jesus convey a radical pacifism is explained away by Aslan, who maintains that his teachings—such as the Sermon on the Mount—are the creation of his followers in an effort to convince the Roman authorities that Christians should not be regarded as a threat to society.

Christian Faith in Our Time

According to the biblical scholar John Dominic Crossan, Jesus' teaching concerning the kingdom of God evokes "an ideal vision of political and religious power, of how this world here below would be run if God, not Caesar, sat on the imperial throne . . . . It includes especially a basic, fundamental, radical, utopian, counter-cultural, or eschatological rejection of the world as it is currently run."[5] This view of the kingdom of God is far removed from the notion that Christianity is about "a pie in the sky by-and-by." There is no doubt that Jesus' message places us in the midst of life, confronted with economic and political realities that demand a heightened religious and ethical response.

It is not likely that Jesus was offering an alternative political system that could be implemented here and now. He was a prophet, speaking truth to power by lifting up a vision of an alternative order that captured the true nature of Israel; he was calling his people to be a light to the world, committed to a more just and compassionate economic and political order. But there are Christians who regard Jesus' message of the kingdom as a call to a more radical response. Brian McLaren, for example, sees Jesus calling his followers to a resistance movement, not a call to arms but a nonviolent resistance of the Spirit which was the only ultimate answer to the demonic character of Roman imperialism—or to imperialism of any kind.

> If this world is indeed the creation of a good, holy, compassionate, wise, and just God, and if it has been conquered and occupied by this destructive, unholy, merciless, tyrannical, stupid, and devious system . . . then Jesus came to launch an insurgency to overthrow that occupying regime. Its goal is to resist the occupation, liberate the planet, and retrain and restore humanity to its original vocation and potential.[6]

As John Updike notes above, there is a remarkable inversion of values in Jesus' message. It reflects his sensitivity to the warped values of his society, dominated as it was by the wealthy elite and a corrupt religious establishment.[7] This sensitivity is also expressed, and quite remarkably, in the kind

---

5. Crossan, *The Essential Jesus*, 7–8.
6. McLaren, *Everything Must Change*, 128–29.
7. The notion that the Jewish people as a whole were mortal enemies of Jesus and responsible for his execution has been a fateful, tragic development in western history. It is the language of John's gospel in particular that has inspired this charge. His account of Jesus' death reflects both a greater distance in time from the event than that of the other Gospels, and also the particular situation faced by the community in which John was living. It was marked by considerable tension and animosity between Christians and Jews,

of life he chose to live; he was consistently associating with the poor and with people of questionable character on the margins of society. He often sat at table and shared a meal with them, which was seen as an intimate act of acceptance. This latter practice was particularly offensive to the Pharisees ("see how he eats with sinners and tax collectors"), for whom the essence of religion was maintaining one's purity through strict adherence to the law. For Jesus, far more important than the rules and regulations of the law was the state of one's inner life. The law focused on external observances, while one's inner life was the source of moral action. He summoned his hearers to love God and to reach out to the neighbor with a compassionate spirit (Matt 22:36–40).

Jesus' vision of the imminent kingdom of God shaped this radical nature of his moral teachings—what scholars refer to as the eschatological character of his message (from the Greek word *eschaton*, referring to the end time). In other words, Jesus sensed the coming of the end to the Jewish story as his contemporaries knew it, and the prospect of judgment. His reference to an imminent end of things has prompted endless debates on how to understand him. Several prominent views include the belief that he was simply mistaken about the time of the end (which would not be surprising since he attributes that knowledge to the Father alone), but was conveying a truth concerning the reality of judgment in whatever form it might take. Another view is that he was referring to the fall of Jerusalem, which occurred in 70 CE and which brought a catastrophic end to the temple-centered religion of the Jewish people. In any event, the urgency of the kingdom of God in Jesus' teaching has carried explosive power in the lives of many Christians in every generation, with the abiding truth that we are to consciously live our lives with the sense that "the end is nigh, be faithful in all that you do."

The sense of urgency in Jesus' ethic places the listener in an immediate, one-to-one relation to the neighbor, with all other relations and obligations, which complicate the moral decisions we make, falling aside. Jesus urged his hearers to seize the moment, to manifest the kingdom of God by acting selflessly on behalf of their neighbor. He makes it particularly clear that God's forgiveness is inseparable from one's own willingness to forgive one's neighbor (Mark 11:25, Matt 6:14–15). It is a radical message,

---

encouraging John's tendency to speak disparagingly of "the Jews." The reality, of course, is that Jesus was executed by the Romans in collusion with the priestly class, which felt threatened by the message and popularity of Jesus.

beckoning everyone who hears to a compassionate sensitivity to the needs of others, bringing a healing, reconciling balm to all of one's relationships. If all we knew of Jesus was his ethic of compassion, it alone would guarantee his place as a revered figure in the human story.

The "Wonder Works"

I believe that both the life and message of Jesus convey a powerful authenticity that relates well to the Christian confession that he is the Christ, a man with a divinely bestowed purpose. What we genuinely know of him indicates a remarkable congruence between his life and his message. An important part of this congruence was his devotion to healing those who were physically and mentally afflicted. The people regarded his healings as "wonder works," and we can well regard them as paranormal activity—not fully explainable, but undoubtedly involving the profound impact of his person.

If we choose to call these works "miracles," we introduce conceptual baggage from our own time that likely confuses more than clarifies the subject. The idea that laws of nature were being breached—the usual understanding today of a miracle—does not enter into the sense of wonder expressed by Jesus' contemporaries. According to Scripture there were others as well who were performing wonder works, including his disciples; it was not unique in the culture of that time. The important thing is the distinctive significance or meaning of Jesus' healings. From his own statements, they were pointers to the Spirit of God in their midst.

In considering the wonder works it is important to recognize that biblical faith brings God into the very midst of life as Lord of both history and nature. The divine power is seen as quite obviously at work in Jesus as a messianic figure, accomplishing its purposes. The kingdom of God expresses this power and presence of God in the midst of life; Jesus' works reveal the will of God, which is compassionate and merciful, bringing acts of healing, life, and renewal. But there is a hidden character to these works of wonder, expressed in the language of John's gospel where they are called *signs*. Their *significance* is not grasped by everyone, indicating that it is faith that truly sees what Jesus is doing and accomplishing with these works. He's not proving anything about himself, for the Gospels make it clear that he is not interested in working wonders as mere displays. Rather, his works are

The Historical Jesus

done and proclaimed in order that people might see and embrace the reign of God in their own lives.

In addition to wonder works of healing there are wonder works of nature in the Gospels, and they call for a different response. The traditional view has been that because Jesus is God in human form, he can perform miracles of any kind. But these natural wonders in which Jesus calms the wind and the waves (Matt 8:23–27), multiplies bread and fishes (Matt 14:15–21), turns water into wine (John 2:1–11), and raises people who are dead (Luke 8:49–56, John 11:43–44), beg for different understandings. I believe that responsible biblical scholarship resists the idea that "miracles" of this kind are proof that Jesus was really divine and consequently completely sovereign over the world of nature. On the contrary, there are more immediate and convincing factors at work in these accounts. The Gospels are full of stories that are written to make a theological point, and I believe we see this happening in these natural wonders. Some may be stories where the historical basis is questionable, while others have been events that were shaped by the writer to make a point concerning the meaning of Jesus or to convey a word of support to his followers.

This last understanding is apparent from interpretations proposed by theologians of the ancient church. The church father Tertullian, for example, in addressing the story of Jesus stilling the waves to rescue his disciples from a sinking boat, turns it into an allegory:

> That little ship presented a figure of the church, in that she is disquieted in the sea, that is, in the world, by the waves, that is, by persecutions and temptations, [with] the Lord patiently sleeping, as it were, until, roused at last by the prayers of the saints, he checks the world and restores tranquility to His own.[8]

To question the factuality of those wonder works related to nature may come as a shock to many Christians. The notion that the truth of Scripture is dependent on factual inerrancy lingers on in fundamentalist churches, and there is also the modern mind-set that brings a scientific outlook to ancient stories, finding no value or legitimate meaning in any event that has not actually occurred. Jesus' contemporaries engaged stories much more imaginatively, especially when related to a dominant figure such as Jesus. Many of those hearing these stories (they were always being told, of course, before eventually being recorded) were convinced by the person of Jesus

---

8. Cited in Richardson, *The Miracle Stories*, 93.

to see the truth of the wonders being told. His authority over every threat we encounter in life is proclaimed in these accounts, even over death itself, with the resurrection clearly in mind. These "events" become the vehicle for conveying the meaning of Jesus, proclaiming the presence of God in his life and ministry.

Other themes of the tradition come into play as well, as in the story of the feeding of the five thousand and turning water into wine, which invite a sacramental understanding. In the former narrative the writer is presenting Jesus himself as the "bread of life" through a story in which everyone is satisfied. That story also makes a connection with some events related in the Old Testament, a common feature of these accounts. The story of Moses and the manna from heaven during the Israelites' wilderness sojourn (Exod 16), and Elisha feeding one hundred men with twenty loaves of barley (2 Kgs 4:42–44), are acts which stand prominently in the background of Jesus feeding the five thousand. The Gospel writers are authenticating the ministry of Jesus by drawing connections with prophets the people recognize from their tradition. The challenge for the contemporary reader is to see these stories both in light of the purpose of the writers, and in view of the ancient mind-set of those who heard them, children of a culture far different from our own.

This chapter has conveyed my conviction that it is important to retrieve the *natural* Jesus in contrast to the *supernatural* Jesus that tends to dominate our consciousness. The story of Jesus of Nazareth is that God is truly at work in his humanity. To be sure, there was something about him that distinguished his life and ministry, making him different from the other wonder workers—perhaps we could say, that conveyed a sense of mystery about him. But it was not until the resurrection that everything became clear. It was as though scales were removed from his followers' eyes and they could now see clearly just who he was. They now saw as they had never seen before the *meaning* of his life, his ministry, and his death on the cross.

Ever since, the Christian claim has been that in this particular human being the presence of the divine has become transparent: God is "for us," God seeks us out, God calls us to a new life patterned after his own. We see in Jesus' life a persuasive expression of the divine in our midst: the God who reaches out to the forsaken, the dispossessed, the lost, and brings healing to the sick and cleansing to those possessed by the demons in their lives. He brought together at the table the marginalized people, the expendable ones, those with no status and little hope in the world. No wonder that his followers saw in his life the embodiment—the incarnation—of the love of God.

Chapter Eight

The Christ of Faith

Jesus is, for us as Christians, the decisive revelation of what a life full of God looks like. Radically centered in God and filled with the Spirit, he is the decisive disclosure and epiphany of what can be seen of God embodied in a human life ... [H]is life incarnates the character of God, indeed, the passion of God. In him we see God's passion.

—Marcus J. Borg[1]

Long before anyone talked about "nature" and "substance," "person" and "Trinity," the early Christians had quietly but definitely discovered that they could say what they felt obliged to say about Jesus (and the Spirit) by telling the Jewish story of God, Israel, and the world in the Jewish language of Spirit, Word, Torah, Presence/Glory, Wisdom, and now Messiah/Son. It is as though they discovered Jesus within the Jewish monotheistic categories they already had. The categories seem to have been made for him. They fitted him like a glove.

—N.T. Wright[2]

---

1. Borg, *The Heart of Christianity*, 88.
2. Borg and Wright, *The Meaning of Jesus*, 163.

The Christ of Faith

As we move from the Jesus of history to the Christ of faith, we encounter a host of biblical metaphors that seek to express the meaning of Jesus. These metaphors are taken originally from the Jewish tradition which nurtured Jesus, metaphors related to the Jewish expectation of a messiah. They are referred to as messianic titles, which I have mentioned here and there in earlier chapters—Son of God, Lamb of God, Light of the World, Good Shepherd, Bread of Life, Alpha and Omega, and many more. Each metaphor conveys a different meaning or nuance that the believing community wants to say about Jesus. It will be helpful to begin by considering two of those metaphors that have been particularly important in expressing the meaning of Jesus.

Jesus, Son of God

The metaphor "Son of God" has assumed a kind of ultimate status in the theology of the church. Its use reflects a development that we've noted about God-talk, in which a transition takes place from metaphorical to metaphysical language. But now this occurs in a quite different context, where we are addressing the mystery of God in the life of a specific human being. I should reemphasize that metaphors convey truth, but not in a literal sense. Their meaning is "to see *as*," which means their truth is understood in a figurative rather than literal manner.[3] To say that Jesus is the Son of God is to see him *as* the Son of God rather than making a simple statement of fact. It is a confessional statement, beyond verification, and making use of a metaphor to acknowledge a mystery beyond our comprehension. On the face of it, this should be more than obvious. "Describing" the divine Mystery in terms of a male family relationship, of father to son, is clearly to use a metaphor. But in the popular mind the metaphor of father and son has been literalized, and the considerable force of tradition over the centuries has legitimized that literal understanding, at least in the minds of most Christians until more recent times.

The Son of God metaphor was a common designation in the Old Testament, where it was used in reference to Israel (Exod 4:22, Hos 11:1), to the king of Israel (2 Sam 7:14, Ps 2:7), and to angels (Job 1:6). The point of these references is to affirm a close relationship between Israel, kings, and angels to God, such as a child to parent, or son to father. It was a way of attributing divine favor to the one so designated. In the story of the virgin

3. Borg and Wright, *The Meaning of Jesus*, 150–53.

birth we see the Son of God idea expressed in a biological metaphor where the Son is conceived by the Spirit of God. It was also an honorific title in the Gentile world, but with a quite different meaning: the Roman Emperor was designated as Son of God, a prestigious title for one who was at the top of a powerful political hierarchy. In light of this fact, calling Jesus the Son of God was a political claim in the eyes of the Empire, putting Christians at considerable political risk. They were often accused of treason.

Thus we must keep in mind that there is a specific tradition that lies behind the biblical language of Son of God, giving a particular meaning to the phrase. The God of the Jews was *Emmanuel*, the God who is "with us," and the climax of God's dwelling with his people was the coming of the messiah, God's "anointed one." In Jesus the messianic Son of God has dwelt among his people, bringing and embodying a message of salvation. Particularly in Matthew's gospel, directed primarily to the Jewish community, there is an obvious intent to see in Jesus' life and ministry the fulfillment of Old Testament prophecies concerning the messiah. Followers of Jesus recognized that for many Jews this claim required a radical re-understanding of messianic expectations. The messiah would not appear as a king who would restore the glory of Israel as in the days of King David, but would come as a "suffering servant" who embodies the kingdom of God in their midst.[4]

Jesus, Word of God

Another metaphor that was particularly powerful in shaping Christian thinking about Jesus—closely related to the Son of God metaphor—was the Greek word *Logos*, which is translated as both "reason" and "word." It functioned in Stoic philosophy as a rational principle that gave order and purpose to the universe. Its use in the Greek translation of the Old Testament (called the "Septuagint") and the Greek New Testament is usually with the meaning of "word" as a form of divine revelation or communication. The most important use of Logos in the New Testament occurs in the first chapter of John, where the author identifies this concept with the

---

4. The servant theme is powerfully expressed in the book of Isaiah, where it appears in chapters 42, 49, 50, 52, and 53. Scholars generally regard the servant as a reference to the nation of Israel, but quite understandably, in light of Jesus' life and his death on the cross, Christians have seen in this description the story of Jesus himself who embodies the redemptive mission of the servant.

The Christ of Faith

God of creation: "In the beginning was the Word, and the Word was with God, and the Word was God. He was in the beginning with God..." (John 1:1-2). This exalted vision of the Word is then identified with Jesus in John 1:14: "And the Word became flesh and dwelt among us, full of grace and truth...."[5] These verses gave rise to a Logos Christology, which exerted a dominant influence in succeeding centuries as the church debated its understanding of Jesus Christ. It fit quite well with the idea of an incarnation, which expresses John's words, "And the Word became flesh."

In rethinking the church's theology, I believe what the church is saying in identifying Jesus with the Logos can be put this way: "Jesus, the Christ, comes to us *as* a Word from God himself; he is a final, decisive message that bestows a human face on the Mystery that is God." With that little word "as," we acknowledge the metaphorical nature of this confession of faith, both in our saying that Jesus is the Word and in referring to God in personal terms. But a different direction was taken in the Christology of the ancient church. As it deliberated on the meaning of Jesus Christ, leading up to the Nicene Creed and the Holy Trinity dogma, the discussion was dominated by the metaphysical concepts of Greek philosophy (as we noted in chapter 5).

Given the nature of the intellectual debate, the church found it necessary to frame the meaning of Jesus in the language of substance, nature, and person, using those terms as a kind of ultimate way of saying who Jesus is (the Son is of the "same substance" as the Father). Either explicitly or implicitly, that language has governed the orthodox Christology of the church ever since.

What Do We Mean by "Incarnation"?

The consequence of the church's deliberations is that both its doctrine of God and its doctrine of Jesus Christ have two sets of languages, the one

---

5. John's use of Logos as a means of interpreting Jesus to the Gentile world was a masterful stroke. A likely figure in the background for his use of Logos was Philo of Alexandria, a contemporary of Jesus. Philo was a Jew whose work is a synthesis of the Old Testament revelation and Greek thought, bringing Moses and Plato together in one philosophical system. God to Philo is utterly transcendent, but governs the world through mediators. The most prominent among them was Logos, who occupied a place between God and human beings, neither uncreated nor created, but a true image of God. Logos was depicted as the "mind" of God, the "shadow" of God, the "firstborn son" of God.

biblical and metaphorical, the other philosophical or metaphysical; the one rooted in the Hebraic tradition, the other in the Greek. These two traditions were at the center of a continuing debate in the decades following 381 CE, when the church officially adopted the Nicene Creed. As we noted, that Creed settled the relation of Jesus to God the Father and the Spirit, resulting in the Holy Trinity teaching. But now the debate continued over how to interpret the fact that Jesus was not simply a man but also in some way divine, a genuine part of the Trinity. What did his relation to the Father and Spirit mean for his own identity? He was God incarnate, but how was that to be understood?

The division between the opposing sides in this debate was determined by each of their starting points. Those who began their interpretation with the divine Logos who became human in Jesus were well on their way to stressing the divinity of Christ, while those who began with the human Jesus who was also divine were bound to stress his humanity. These two strains of thinking about Jesus, the one from the Greek tradition and the other from the Hebraic, are often characterized as beginning "from above," and "from below." There were two schools of Christian theology at the time, each representing one side of this debate. The school in Alexandria, Egypt advocated the Logos Christology, while the school in Antioch, in Asia Minor, espoused a Hebraic approach that began with the historical Jesus.

As the debate came down to the wire, there were those on both sides whose ideas were rejected because they short-changed either the humanity or the divinity of Jesus. The issue was settled at the Council of Chalcedon in 451 CE, with the assertion that Jesus was both "true man and true God." The Council adopted language that had been proposed in the third century by the church father, Tertullian, who had described the "composition" of Jesus as true man and true God: he was one person, undivided, but possessing two distinct natures, one human and one divine. This language from Chalcedon has been a final, governing word for orthodox Christology, functioning as a philosophical expression of what the incarnation is all about.

The Logos idea, with the notion of preexistence, is assumed in the church's idea of incarnation. What was driving this "high" Christology was the conviction that if Jesus was a genuine Savior, he had to come directly from God. That was a major argument of Athanasius (c. 296–373), the church father who was a dominant figure at Nicaea. His concept of salvation was a "divinizing" of the believer by an act of grace, made possible

The Christ of Faith

by Jesus who was divine by nature. It is understandable that this picture of Jesus, "coming down from heaven," created a figure that believers were likely to regard as divine, but clothed in a human body. Though the "true man and true God" language at Chalcedon appears to be even handed, the emphasis clearly lies on his divinity. That is what makes Jesus the unique person he is in the eyes of believers and non-believers alike, the claim that he's not just like the rest of us human beings but is also "divine."

I believe this metaphysical understanding of Jesus poses a crisis for the church's message today. What appeared necessary to say about him in the western cultural world of the fourth and fifth centuries appears simply curious or bizarre to the cultural world of today. Language that was quite acceptable to Christians in a precritical age has become a source of agitation and debate in a post-critical age, posing the task of deconstruction. The problem lies in the metaphysical assumptions that are wedded to the language we use. We have arrived at a time when the church can frankly acknowledge that we do not know what a divine incarnation is. It is an absolutely unique event; we have no means by which to describe it. Given the cultural context of the ancient church, which had become a thoroughly Gentile institution, one can see why it made use of the Greek tradition's metaphysical language. It provided a rational framework that satisfied the quest for understanding, but that framework is no longer viable.

As noted in the quotation above from N. T. Wright, the Jewish cultural and theological world from which the first Christians came had its own language for expressing the meaning of Jesus. It did not use such words as "substance," "nature," and "person," which reflect a quite different, philosophical setting for the understanding of an incarnation. The option remains today to return to biblical language to say what the church needs to say about the meaning of Jesus. The biblical language is obviously metaphorical, encouraging the recognition that we face an absolute mystery in the person of Christ. Christians are those who confess that mystery and who should be willing to acknowledge their poverty in efforts to articulate what it means. In addition to such metaphors as the Bible gives us, there are those that have emerged in the life of the contemporary church—Jesus as "the face of God" or "the heart of God." They are effective expressions for our time in conveying the gospel message.

It is a justifiable concern today that framing the incarnation in metaphysical terms reinforces among the laity a literal, theistic view of the incarnation. Theologians may well acknowledge the mythic character of the statement, "God sent his Son into the world," but generally speaking that understanding is never conveyed to the laity, many of whom are puzzled if not insulted by what they take to be a literal statement. This metaphysical setting reinforces the objectifying of the image of God that poses a considerable burden on the church's theology. Not just the doctrine of God, but the doctrine of the preexisting, virgin-born Son of God needs an explicit change in understanding from metaphysical to metaphorical language.

Finally, the rationalist character of the church's thinking about the incarnation risks losing the reality of the human Jesus. We have in fact made a kind of generic human being out of Jesus, losing our sense of the actual historical person that he was. He has become a metaphysical construct—one undivided person but with two natures—quite removed from the Jesus we know in the Synoptic Gospels. This has made it difficult indeed to recognize the biblical Jesus in the Jesus of the Nicene Creed. Efforts have been made to formulate creeds in contemporary language, and that task will undoubtedly become more urgent in coming years. Such creeds should certainly convey the mystery that we see in Jesus, but in terms that relate him to the redeeming purposes of God without inviting a presumptuous speculation about his personal being. What is essential is that our confessions of faith capture the uniqueness and wonder of Jesus as that One in whom the wonder of God's love is embodied.

"God Was in Christ"

Between the alternatives of a Christology "from above" and "from below," I am clearly taking the latter route. This does not mean, however, that we repeat the thinking of those who took that path in the ancient church, which would be neither desirable nor possible. Nor is it the understandable resistance to the notion of a member of the Godhead entering the world from a heavenly realm; that imagery can be received for what it is, a metaphorical or mythical expression of the meaning of Jesus. The reason, rather, is that we have come to know Jesus as a historical figure through the New Testament Gospels, which means that the responsible avenue toward understanding him is to begin at that point. Admittedly, the Jesus we encounter there is the post-Easter Jesus, but with the help of biblical scholarship we can discern an authentic human Jesus in the Synoptic Gospels. In light of the gospel he proclaimed, the image of God embedded in his message, and the stunning conclusion of his life in resurrection, we are moved to believe that God is uniquely present in his life.

An important part of this recognition for Christians, though not often observed, is the fact that Jesus embodies a profound sense of the true and the good concerning the human story. A serious engagement with his life and message brings the fundamental belief that who we are as human beings and what we ought to be is revealed in his life. It is not a life that he achieved through extraordinary moral effort in order to earn the favor of God, but a life that reflects the grace of God, a life that we receive as God's gift to us. His reaching out with compassion and healing to the poor and marginalized in society, the sick and afflicted, reveals an ethic of love that points us to the God of love. The model of his life places us on a path—"the Way," as the early Christians expressed it—in which we relate not just our own lives but all of life and creation to the God revealed in Jesus. To know the Truth in this context is to be "in" the Truth, to be transformed by that Truth in the sense of receiving life anew through what Jesus, in his life, death, and resurrection, has come to mean for us.

This conviction that Jesus brings God to us is stated by the Apostle Paul: "God was in Christ, reconciling the world to himself" (2 Cor 5:19). In other words, we see in Christ one who is carrying out a divine mission in the world, a divine purpose that we can discern in light of the messianic setting that informs our thinking about Jesus. The character of his life, his teaching, his crucifixion and resurrection, all confirm for the believer that indeed "God was in Christ." This recognition leads to a viable understanding of the meaning of Jesus as God incarnate: Jesus incarnates the will and purpose of God within the human story; he *embodies* that will of God, revealing what Marcus Borg in the initial quote above refers to as the "character" and the "passion" of God, or the "heart" of God.

These metaphors convey the meaning of the gospel, the "good news" that God is love, the God who is well beyond our comprehension is "for us." It means that in the person of Jesus we are directly addressed by God. We find in him that peace that passes all understanding, an ultimate hope in the midst of despair, a source of meaning and purpose where life threatens to be meaningless and without purpose. We see embodied in his life and ministry, his crucifixion and resurrection, the fulfillment of the Old Testament vision of Emmanuel, God with us. He brings the promise of new life that stretches even to the grave.

To those wedded to the language of metaphysics, this understanding of incarnation will not be sufficient. The "essence" of God in Jesus—the *homoousios*, or "same substance" according to the rational framework of the Nicene Creed—is missing, and therefore they believe that it cannot be a real incarnation. The revelation in Jesus of that God who is love, who brings reconciliation, peace, hope, meaning, and direction to our lives, is a bogus revelation if Jesus is not the God of metaphysics. I am contending that such a view says both too much and too little; it seeks to give us a philosophical foundation or explanation of an absolute mystery, which is impossible, and its language fails to convey to our contemporaries a clear gospel message. If we are to speak of the *essence* of God, let it be the very heart of God whom Jesus reveals and embodies in his life and teaching.

To remain with the language of the Bible, we can locate the mystery of Jesus in the Spirit of God rather than categories of Greek philosophy. To say that Jesus embodies the will and purpose of God is to say that the Spirit of God is carrying out a divine mission in and through his life and ministry, his death and resurrection. This is the testimony of faith rather than a rational argument that would explain the incarnation. It does not remove the offense of the gospel, but rather shifts it from Jesus as a combination God-man to Jesus as that particular person in whom God is accomplishing his purposes. *Jesus is the decisive revelation of God and a transformative presence in the human story. That is his uniqueness, his "otherness" in relation to everyone else.* In this view Jesus is truly one of us, *really* a human being, possessing the same DNA as the rest of us, at the same time as he is truly other than us in his God-given role as the one who brings and embodies God's good news.

Dare we speculate about the inner life of Jesus as the one who fulfills this remarkable mission of God? Can we ask what it may have been about his life that made him the sole, exclusive instrument in the hands of God? To raise this question runs the risk of saying more than we possibly can about Jesus. Only if we recognize the purely hypothetical nature of such an attempt, and only if it serves to edify and illumine the life of faith, would it be worth the effort. I believe these conditions are met reasonably well in the reflections of the biblical theologian Donald Baillie.[6] He understands the "otherness" of Jesus in terms of divine grace; God initiates, Jesus responds, and within that dynamic, divine grace fully embraces Jesus and makes him who he is. He lives a grace-filled life, one marked by complete trust in God.

6. Baillie, *God Was in Christ*.

The Christ of Faith

As such he becomes a perfect instrument in God's hands, fulfilling a divine, redemptive purpose.

Baillie makes clear that Jesus' mission is not the result of his earning adoption by God due to an exemplary life, but the result of divine grace that achieves its purpose in him. Baillie thus begins from below with the humanity of Jesus, and incorporates a from-above dimension in terms of God's prevenient grace. This is his alternative to a Logos figure that enters this life from a heavenly realm through a virgin birth. I believe it is an alternative that is much more promising in reaching people today. Jesus is God's man, totally removed from the rest of us in his God-given mission, but as creatures who also live and thrive by God's grace, we recognize him as one of us.

Chapter Nine

The Cross and Resurrection

God reveals his power through weakness, his heights through lowliness, his wisdom through foolishness.... The defining feature of Christianity, that which sets it apart from paganism and a merely natural knowledge of God, is the cross, something that is neither visible to the senses nor understandable to reason but that is accessible only to faith.

—John Caputo[1]

The real question in regard to the resurrection is not whether we believe it to be an historical and scientific fact, but whether we "trust" in the resurrection. The former is a question that cannot be answered in a scientific or rational way; the latter is an experiential question directed to one's faith.

—Diana Butler Bass[2]

In this chapter I want to elaborate on two events that are essential to the conviction that "God was in Christ." Though understood as two occurrences, they are inseparable—the cross and resurrection. Turning first to the cross, it is the defining event in Jesus' life. All of the Gospel writers

---

1. Caputo, "Toward a Postmodern Theology of the Cross," 213.
2. Bass, *Christianity after Religion*, 129.

The Cross and Resurrection

give a disproportionate amount of space to that final week leading up to the crucifixion, and that is because it crystallizes the meaning of his life and the meaning of the gospel message he proclaimed. His death brings to a climax the whole direction of his life, which bore a cruciform character from the very beginning of his ministry. He was opposed and rejected by his own people (Luke 4:16–30), led the wearying life of an itinerant ("the Son of Man has nowhere to lay his head"), and had to cope with the opposition of the dominant religious and political powers of his day that collaborated in his execution. From early on that character of his life, together with his bloody execution, led his followers to see in him "a lamb led to the slaughter," a sacrificial death that was "for us," bringing atonement between humanity and God.

In this way the cross became a symbolic act, and the most obvious metaphor to convey its meaning for followers raised in the Jewish tradition was that of a sacrifice.[3] At the beginning of Jesus' ministry, the Gospel of John pictures John the Baptist calling him "the lamb of God that takes away the sin of the world" (John 1:29). The offering of animal sacrifice was a prominent ritual act not only in Judaism but throughout the ancient world, including Greece and Rome. It seems to have been an innate response to the mystery of life, with its religious power coming from the conviction that in offering one's sacrifice to God one is sanctifying oneself. Whether it is seen as a sin offering or one of worship and thanksgiving, it is the symbolic offering of oneself that gives the sacrifice its religious meaning.

The New Testament letter to the Hebrews pictures Jesus as a perfect sacrifice "for us," which could reflect a conviction that had become common among Jews during the Maccabean era (second and first centuries BCE). During that bloody time of revolt, the deaths of many "righteous martyrs" came to be seen as expiatory, that is, covering the sins of the people. The Apostle Paul takes up the theme of sacrifice but also transforms it with his exhortation to the Christians in Rome to "present your bodies as a living sacrifice . . ." (Rom 12:1), an offering to God. For Christians, sacrifice was now a matter of offering up oneself to God in the spirit of Jesus Christ.

---

3. For a helpful work on the subject of sacrifice in the Christian context, see Young, *Sacrifice and the Death of Christ*.

Theories of the Atonement

Beyond this notion of the cross as a sacrifice "for our sins," there are several interpretations of the cross's meaning that over the years have been prominent in the church's theology—we call them "theories of the atonement." An atonement metaphor that was popular for almost a thousand years was that of a ransom. It was inspired by a number of biblical verses, such as Mark 10:45, where Jesus says, "For the Son of man also came . . . to give his life as a ransom for many." Humanity is in bondage, held hostage by the devil. In this highly imaginative theory, God offers Jesus as a ransom to the devil without his knowing that Jesus was the Son of God. Just as the devil had tricked Adam and Eve in the garden of Eden, so now God tricks him, with death on the cross followed by the victory of resurrection. The devil was a very real figure in the ancient imagination, encouraging the idea of an epic struggle between God and the Evil One. Life, after all, was an ongoing struggle between good and evil.

Not until the eleventh century did another theory of the atonement supersede the ransom theory. Anselm (1033–1109), the Archbishop of Canterbury and an influential theologian, became impatient with notions of divine trickery in the ransom theory, proposing a view that was more in tune with the feudal society of his time. God is seen as a medieval king to whom we owe obedience and honor. Because we are in bondage to sin we cannot give the honor to God that he deserves; we are indebted to God and can never satisfy that debt. It places us under judgment, which is the human situation. The church's penitential system informs this theory, where in addition to repentance and forgiveness, a penance is required to satisfy the debt we owe to God. Because Jesus is God he can meet that debt, and because he is human he can do it on our behalf. Thus his death satisfies the honor that humanity owes to God.

A late contemporary of Anselm, Abelard (1079–1142), took issue with the archbishop over the satisfaction motif that dominates his theory. Must God's honor be satisfied before he can be merciful? Is this the God of Scripture, who cannot forgive without being appeased by a gruesome death? Abelard did not work out a complete alternative theory to that of Anselm, but his stress fell on the love of God that is exemplified in the cross. That love has the power to influence the sinner, bringing one to repentance. This focus on the meaning of the cross in terms of its impact on the subjectivity of the sinner has led to its designation as the "subjective" or "moral influence" theory of the atonement. It did not displace the view of Anselm, which remained dominant for several centuries, but it has persisted at the margins of atonement theology to the present time.

The idea of satisfying God was retained but took on a different thrust in the theology of Thomas Aquinas (1225-1274), the patron saint of Roman Catholic theology, and John Calvin (1509-1564), a major Reformer in the Protestant Reformation. Instead of the honor of God, Aquinas and Calvin see the demands of a just God as needing to be satisfied. The Apostle Paul's emphasis on justification of the sinner stands in the background of this view, but now with a strong legal, courtroom character where the accused sinner is acquitted by God the Judge on account of the righteousness of Jesus. The punishment deserved by the sinner is redirected to Jesus on our behalf. In this view, the words "for us" mean "in our place," a literal substitution where Jesus receives the punishment that we deserve with his death on the cross. This "penal" theory, as Calvin called it, has been dominant in Protestantism and Catholicism throughout the modern period.[4]

A view proposed by a Swedish Lutheran theologian of the twentieth century, Gustaf Aulen, puts emphasis on the victory of the cross and resurrection. In his book entitled *Christus Victor*, Aulen sought to recapture the victory motif which he saw in the ancient ransom theory and in the theology of Martin Luther. As a twentieth-century theologian he does not picture this cosmic struggle as a vanquishing of the devil as such, but as a victory over demonic forces, the powers of evil that have enslaved humankind. The outcome is not the satisfaction of God but the victory God carries through in the cross and resurrection. Aulen's view brings a strong cosmic scope to its understanding of the divine victory, and certainly greater stress is placed on the resurrection than it receives in the other theories.

Problems in Atonement Theology

There are few doctrines that have occasioned such a variety of diverse views as the doctrine of the atonement. One can understand this in light of the depth of meaning that can be plumbed in the event of the cross, but I believe it is more than that. The nature of the subject is so entwined with its original culture and religious tradition that it poses a challenge for the church's theology in every succeeding historical era and cultural setting. How the cross is an act of atonement and how it is "for you" constitutes a

---

4. For an engaging account of the atonement theories, placed in a dialogue setting, see Lose, *Making Sense of the Cross*.

hermeneutical challenge for every generation. F. D. Maurice, an English theologian of the nineteenth century, relates a hypothetical incident that illustrates the problem: a man was sitting on a pier, fishing, when he heard someone running behind him. Turning, he gasped as the runner leaped off the end of the pier. After a few moments it was clear that he had drowned. The fisherman then heard a voice crying, "He died for you!"

Maurice is making the point that our contemporaries are as mystified about the death of Christ as was the fisherman about the death he had just witnessed. At the root of the problem, I believe, is that the church's theology of atonement has failed to convey a clear gospel message. The dominant theories come across as transactions that have to be made in order for God to accept the sinner. The practice of sacrifice itself can be distorted into an act of appeasement or propitiation of an angry God, a kind of bribe to gain a desired action from God. The distinguishing mark of these transactional atonement theories is to make the death of Christ a *satisfaction* of God's demands, whose honor or justice must be met before we hear the gospel. In one sense this character of atonement theology is quite understandable; atonement as reconciliation presupposes a ruptured relationship between two parties, and mending that relationship does involve "making things right" between them. Making that happen is bound to be painful because it involves recognition of guilt in injuring or destroying that relationship.

Since God cannot be at fault in this damaged relationship, he is pictured as the aggrieved party who now requires his "pound of flesh." Jesus on the cross is the victim of this demand. He pays the debt of honor, or suffers the punishment "for us," which he can do because he is the incarnate God. An obvious problem in these transactions is that God in heaven is divorced from God on the cross; the former God is the personification of holiness and the law, the latter of suffering love and the gospel. The result is two Gods, with the cross serving as the means of reconciling them. This is not the message of the New Testament, where "God so loved the world that he gave his son . . ." and where "God was in Christ, reconciling the world . . . ." It is the one God who loves and suffers on our behalf, bringing forgiveness and reconciliation into the world in the face of human fallenness, alienation, and estrangement.

There is also a shadow side to these satisfaction views of the cross that many find troubling. Crucifixion is a violent, bloody means of execution, and these theories present this event as the means that God takes in order to "make things right." In order to emphasize the price that Jesus paid, the cross is often dramatized in a way that glorifies the suffering and agony that he experienced on the cross. Mel Gibson's film *The Passion of the Christ* comes to mind as an extreme example. The intent is to arouse feelings of guilt and contrition as we contemplate the cross, but as an act intended, even designed, by God it conveys the message that violence is the prerequisite to serving a divine purpose. The suffering of Christ also becomes problematic in these satisfaction theories, where his agony on the cross is the consequence of a divine requirement. The religious force of the cross depends on its not being the satisfaction of a requirement but an act of self-sacrifice: "He laid down his life . . . ."

The satisfaction theories, with all of their questionable features, are also guilty of creating a big picture that presumes too much about what the cross means in the mind of God. It is another example of the excessive claims of orthodox theology, drawing inferences that move well beyond the witness of Scripture. The orthodox concern is that the cross must be understood as an event that has more than a subjective impact on the believer—the weakness it sees in the view of Abelard. It must also be an act that literally changes the mind of God in his relation to humanity. In other words, the cross must bring a metaphysical change, an "objective" change that makes a difference in God's disposition toward the sinner and the subsequent course of history. This view encourages the separation of the cross from the life and ministry of Jesus; it becomes an isolated act that in itself would define the gospel. This in turn accentuates the problematic character of a gospel that is based on a transactional cross.

The Meaning of the Cross

The atonement transaction theologies have inspired many expressions of Christian piety over the centuries, but the theology behind them is not only questionable but is severely handicapped in speaking to people today. The theme of atonement, "at-one-ment," bringing God and humanity together in reconciliation, is certainly an essential part of the Christian message, but *that message needs to be recast in order to transform the cross from a transaction to a divine initiative that expresses the suffering love of God.* The following points can help us in achieving that goal:

1. The cross exposes the evil of human pride, particularly in its corporate expression, as a defenseless Jesus is crushed by the religious and

political powers of his time. Given the prophetic nature of his ministry, challenging the religious establishment and bringing a sharp eye to its hypocrisy, it was predictable that his life would lead to disaster. Thus a man who preached and lived the virtues of compassion and nonviolence suffers a violent death.

2. The cross speaks to our imagination, encouraging the recognition that we all share the kind of self-righteous, all-too-human indignation of the crowd that leads to the condemnation of the innocent. Thus the cross would bring about our own moment of truth in which we recognize ourselves in those who clamored for Jesus' execution. This is to recognize the holiness of God that holds us accountable, as well as the love of God that would move us to repentance.

3. The cross brings a message of forgiveness in the midst of evil ("Father, forgive them for they know not what they do," Luke 23:34), revealing the love of God in Jesus' life that overcomes evil with a reconciling spirit. The cycle of violence and revenge, evil done and evil returned, is broken by the cross. In the warped world in which we live, forgiveness that brings healing and reconciliation is a most powerful expression of love. Both in his life and his death, Jesus demonstrates the love of God, a revelation whose impact throughout the course of history has been far more than we can comprehend. Whatever the inadequacies of atonement theology, the gift of the cross remains wherever it is received with a contrite heart.

4. The cross reveals the suffering love of God, not as an isolated event but as the epitome of Jesus' life and ministry. It was a sacrificial event in the sense that Jesus did not resist his execution or flee from it, but gave himself up to a corrupt religious establishment and a cynical imperial power, going to his death "as a lamb to the slaughter." The Synoptic Gospels convey a sense of the immense struggle this involved for Jesus ("Father, if you are willing, remove this cup from me," Luke 22:42), including his utter sense of abandonment on the cross ("My God, my God, why have you forsaken me?" Matt 27:46). The drama of the cross is powerfully expressed in this excruciating moment, where the self-giving love of this servant of God goes to its depths. Here is the end result of Emmanuel, "God with us" in the person of Jesus, sharing our lives even unto death.

5. Finally, the cross presents a profound example for Christians to follow, epitomizing "the Way" that one sees in the whole shape of Jesus' life. The cross summons the followers of Christ to take up their own cross (Matt 16:24–25), to live their lives with the same spirit of love and self-giving that they see in Jesus. Thus we receive the cross as both a gift and a challenge, a symbol of divine love that suffers for us and with us, and summoning us to live in the spirit of that love in all of our relationships.

The above five points convey an important truth: the meaning of Christ's death on the cross is not to be found in some cosmic event that determines the destiny of the world's inhabitants, whether it poses as a victory over the devil and the powers of evil, the satisfaction of God's honor, or the removal of divine punishment. Rather than to say that it is God on the cross, which has invited considerable misunderstanding, it is God in the life and mission of Jesus Christ, suffering with him from beginning to end. The cross captures and sharpens in one final event the meaning of Jesus' life and ministry. His whole life is *for us,* revealing the meaning of our lives in light of divine love, a love that reaches out to convict, to forgive, to transform, and to empower each of us who responds in faith and devotion. Thus the meaning of the cross is to be found in the personal response of the individual, but it does not stop there. The gospel message brings people together, creating a community in which the God we know in Christ is worshiped and proclaimed, bringing witness of the good news to every corner of the globe.

The Resurrection

For the Christian, one cannot speak of the cross without speaking of the resurrection, and yet in their meanings they are as different as night and day. The crucifixion was a public event, visible to anyone in the neighborhood of Golgotha—the execution site, the place of "the skull"—just outside of Jerusalem. On the other hand, the resurrection is cloaked in mystery, a sign of profound transformation. How are we to understand it? Should we treat it as a metaphor, with Jesus bringing "new life," a new beginning to our lives? Or was the resurrection a historical event? Was the risen Jesus a corpse that returned to life and got out of the tomb? These are perennial questions that would appear to deserve straightforward answers, and yet, they are simply incapable of being answered in a way that is convincing to everyone who asks them. They raise complicated issues that require at the very least an understanding of what is meant by a resurrection in the religious tradition of the disciples and the emerging church.

By Jesus' time the resurrection had become an important feature of Jewish eschatology (from the Greek word *eschaton,* meaning "the end" or "last times"). The idea, at least, appears a few centuries earlier in a memorable metaphor in the book of Ezekiel, where the prophet imagines dry bones that miraculously come to life in portraying God's promise of restoration from exile and new life for his people (Ezek 37:1–14). By Jesus' time the Pharisees were treating it literally as people rising from the dead. In Christian thought the resurrection is pictured as a transformational event that inaugurates a new age—"a new heaven and a new earth." It is clear from the Apostle Paul's correspondence (see 1 Cor 15), which is the earliest reflections we have on this subject, that he understood the presence of Jesus following his death in light of a general resurrection at the end of history. Without that conviction he presumably was at a loss to account for the reality of his own experience on the road to Damascus (Acts 9) where he was confronted by the living Christ.

On the basis of Paul's reflections, which say nothing about an empty tomb, one can hardly conclude that resurrection is the same as the resuscitation of a corpse, where a dead person returns to his physical existence until he dies again. It is fair to say, with theologian John Macquarrie, that "Paul did not equate the resurrection of Jesus with anything so naïve as the belief that the dead body had come alive again."[5] But the idea of resuscitation can be seen as a way of trying to make sense of what had happened, even though resurrection itself carries a quite different meaning; it expresses the goal of history in a final, transformative event. Given the nature of the Gospel accounts, I believe this resurrection faith is the appropriate setting for understanding what happened between Jesus and the disciples. Faith sees his resurrection as an eschatological event in the midst of history, and this encounter of the future in the midst of the present creates the unusual character of the post-resurrection appearances.

The language of the Apostle Paul is helpful. He expresses the transformation connected with resurrection by speaking of "a spiritual body" in contrast to "a physical body" (1 Cor 15:44), a paradox that I think sheds light on what the Gospels portray. Their descriptions of Jesus do reveal a

---

5. Macquarrie, *Jesus Christ in Modern Thought,* 66.

paradoxical situation. At times he is no longer a part of this world, passing through closed doors and journeying with two of his followers on the road to Emmaus without even being recognized (Luke 24:13–35). At other times he is physically present, as when he presents his wounded body to Thomas in order to overcome his doubt. It is a curious mixture of the spiritual and the physical in the risen Christ, but that can be seen as reflecting the mystery of resurrection in the midst of our mortal existence. Jesus as the resurrected one is no longer a part of this world, but the disciples, confronted with his presence, must "certify" his reality in physical terms. This resulted in stories designed to confirm the physical presence of Jesus as a way of testifying to the reality of their experience.

This conclusion, in which resurrection is contrasted to the notion of Jesus getting out of his tomb, is obviously contrary to the traditional view. Traditionalists make their case by arguing a strict "either/or" between the objective event in which Jesus arose from the tomb, and the subjective experience of the disciples. The implication is that the resurrection cannot rest on such a weak basis as the subjectivity of the disciples—something physical really had to happen to Jesus. I would argue that it is impossible to claim a resurrection apart from faith; the objectivity of the resurrection rests in the subjectivity or experience of the disciples, with their belief that something really "happened" in their encounter with the risen Christ.

In whatever way we choose to think about the disciples' experience, perhaps a vision or some kind of encounter, they clearly were overwhelmed by the reality of Jesus' presence. Given the character of the New Testament witness, it is difficult to deny the genuineness of whatever happened; their witness, together with all that followed, gives little credence to the idea that it was a ruse, some kind of conspiracy, or a mass psychosis. For Christians ever since, to believe in the resurrection is to unite themselves with the disciples in their conviction that "Jesus lives!" It is to know the risen Christ in one's own life of discipleship, the one to whom one prays as the living presence of God among us. Poet Christian Wiman states our situation with typical clarity: "Christ's life is not simply a model for how to live, but the living truth of my own existence. Christ is not alive now because he rose from the dead two thousand years ago. He rose from the dead two thousand years ago because he is alive right now."[6]

It is essential to recognize that resurrection does not function as a rational principle that would *explain* the appearances of Jesus. Rather, it is

---

6. Wiman, *My Bright Abyss*, 165.

a word that expresses the mystery of Christ's presence beyond his death, a word that is utterly unique to our historical experience and consequently not something we can understand. The modernist mentality among Christians will insist on a rational basis for the resurrection claim, which results in treating the risen Christ as the resuscitated Christ, a "real," flesh and blood creature like the rest of us. On the contrary, Jesus' resurrection is not an empirical fact accessible to everyone; it is not a datum that could be uncovered by historical investigation. Rather, it captures the Christian hope of a future transformation, and that hope prompts the notion of a transformed Jesus as the way of conveying the experience of the disciples. It is the same Jesus the disciples knew before, but a different Jesus from what he was. He is now the glorified Jesus, known only to faith.

The meaning of the resurrection, then, is found in the lives of Jesus' followers from ancient times to the present, who live with faith in their risen Lord. That faith rests in the God whom Jesus called "Father," who is sovereign over life and death. Another way in which faith expresses the presence of the risen Christ is to speak of the Spirit of God, whom Jesus promised as a Counselor who would maintain his presence, dwelling "with us and in us" (John 14:16–17). Thus the resurrection of Jesus is a final word for people of faith as they contemplate the Mystery of God. Jesus is the one who embodies that Mystery, and who informs and guides all of our thinking about the divine presence in our lives. In light of this, we are bold to use the metaphors, "Son of God" and "Word of God," referring to the resurrected one who is at the center of our relation to God.

In the wake of the resurrection, the early church began to soar with its use of metaphorical language concerning Jesus. Often this was prompted by particular threats in the spiritual and religious environment of the time. A good example is Paul's letter to the Colossians (likely written by one of his disciples), who were being tempted by an appealing, syncretistic mix of Jewish and pagan ideas that posed as legitimate Christian teaching. The writer perceived that it was undermining the place of Jesus in the gospel message, and he responds forcefully with language that the situation demanded. Jesus is "the image of the invisible God" (1:15), and "in him dwells the whole fullness of deity bodily" (2:9). In exalting Jesus with these metaphors he was responding to the philosophical setting he was addressing, with words that both the congregation and his adversaries could not fail to understand. It was language justified by the resurrection faith, and suited to the situation he was facing. It was inferential language, based on his conviction that "God was in Christ."

Sin and Salvation

The cross and resurrection are intimately related to two other concepts in Christian theology, sin and salvation. *Sin* is a religious as well as moral term in which the evil in human life is seen as a rupture in our relation to God, resulting in sinful acts of disobedience. That situation or condition of humanity in the Jewish and Christian traditions goes back to the story of the Fall in the book of Genesis, chapter 3—Adam and Eve in the garden of Eden. The intent of the story is to answer a fundamental question posed by human existence: Why is life like this? What accounts for the evil in the world? Thus it is a mythic story that brings insight into the nature of temptation, placing it in the context of our relation to God.

In the course of history that myth has been treated as a historical event, with profound consequences. In Christian theology the fall is seen as having radically changed human nature from a primeval innocence to a "fallen," corrupt nature, which in turn accounts for the checkered history of humankind. The church's doctrine of original sin, seen as a consequence of the fall, expresses this deeply rooted character of the human problem. Despite the flawed character of its original formulation by Augustine, in which he understood the transmission of an original fallenness through the sexual act from generation to generation, it does convey an obvious insight. The doctrine asserts that our human predicament is not just a matter of making occasional mistakes or errors in moral judgment, but rather reflects a self-centered orientation that brings a self-serving bias to our relationships and blinds us to our own imperfections. Whether relatively benign or highly destructive, sin brings its consequences in our relation to God and to neighbor. Our self-centeredness gets in the way of contrition and repentance, and we do not hesitate to treat others as means to our own ends. To recognize and acknowledge these dynamics in our lives is the first step to fruitful self-knowledge.

In spite of its value in shedding insight into the human character at both the individual and corporate level, the function of original sin in Christian theories of atonement has been quite unfortunate. Combined with the historical view of the fall, the themes of sin and judgment have come to dominate the human story. We are all "children of Adam" who share his guilt and deserve his punishment. The German word for original sin conveys this understanding more vividly: *Erbsünde,* meaning "inherited sin." As sinners under judgment, salvation becomes an act of rescue from the jaws of hell. We can appreciate the insight of the Genesis myth, but we must challenge the implications that the church has drawn from it—the result of mistakenly turning a myth into a historical event.[7] Instead of creating a historical transaction in which God is satisfied, we need to focus on the personal realities of the individual who encounters the gospel in the cross of Christ.

This person-centered view of the impact of the cross does not mean that its meaning is "reduced" to the inner experience of the believer, a charge often made by conservative theologians. Their point is that if the cross is not seen as an objective, history-changing event in itself, quite apart from the believer's response to it, then it is not an objective, saving work of God. This view is simply a way of affirming the validity of a big picture concept of the cross. Insisting on the objectivity of what the cross means does not justify the speculation we see in atonement theory. If the cross is to express the gospel message, then we see it as the ultimate expression of the suffering love of God, revealed in the life of Jesus and coming to a dramatic conclusion in his death and resurrection. When that message reaches the mind and heart of the believer, one is moved to believe that God is "for us," bestowing hope in the face of death itself.

From a Christian perspective, recognizing our "fallen nature"—the fact that we are a problem to ourselves—is not just the mark of honesty and maturity; it is the first step on the way to a new life, being renewed and placed on "the Way" of Jesus' followers. The customary Christian language for this happening is being "saved," but that word typically reflects big-picture thinking where "saved" means rescued from damnation. That meaning seriously cripples a rich biblical term. To make this point does not mean that there is no place for sin and judgment in the Christian message. The

---

7. The traditional understanding of the fall and original sin has of course drawn the critique of many Christian philosophers and theologians in our time, as in this comment of Paul Ricoeur: "The harm that has been done to souls during the centuries of Christianity, first by the literal understanding of the story of Adam and then by the confusion of this myth, treated as history, with later speculations about original sin, will never be adequately told. In asking the faithful to confess belief in this mythic-speculative mass and to accept it as a self-sufficient explanation, the theologians have unduly required a *sacrificium intellectus* [sacrifice of the mind] where what was needed was to awaken believers to a symbolic superintelligence [insight/understanding] of their actual condition." See Ricoeur, *The Symbolism of Evil,* 239.

point, rather, is not to let those realities define and dominate God's relation to the human family. To do that turns the gospel into a "Plan B" on the part of God in rescuing at least a small segment of the human population (those who believe). But apart from that framing story, human sinfulness is certainly obvious to believers. It leaves our relationships broken and brings a sense of estrangement that can drive us to despair. God's judgment is all around us, often graphically seen in the hard truth that "you reap whatever you sow" (Gal 6:7).

I've mentioned that knowing God in the Christian context means knowing oneself, a truth which applies directly to the subject of salvation. For me to know God in Christ involves a reorientation concerning myself, recognizing my brokenness and confessing dependence on divine forgiveness and mercy, knowing God as a God of love and grace, seeing Christ in my neighbor, recognizing human life as a calling to servanthood, and much more. The Greek word *metanoia* is often referred to in speaking of this new life in Christ. It is translated as repentance, but not simply in the sense of being sorry for a sin of disobedience. It conveys the larger meaning of "a change of mode in thought and feeling," the reorientation of one's life and being put on a new path. Salvation is well expressed in the phrase, "coming to one's moment of truth," whether that moment is one overpowering experience (what is often called a "conversion") or is spread in an incremental way over a period of time—perhaps years.

All of this is what we mean by a "saved" life, the kind of life that conveys a spirit of gratitude rooted in the good news of Jesus Christ and growing in the richness of that life. The word *salvation* comes from the Latin word *salvus*, meaning "whole," "sound," and "healed." Returning to that root meaning is helpful in spelling out the meaning of salvation for the Christian life. Being made whole is an act or process of spiritual healing that recognizes the broken, fragmented character of the self-centered life, and looks for new direction in the life and teaching of Jesus.

A particularly significant gift of the cross of Christ is its recasting of the picture of God for Christian faith. The common picture is that of God as the distant monarch who rules from above, and the fatherhood of God has been too easily united with that picture. What the cross does in sharpening the impact and meaning of Jesus' life is to place the reality of God in the midst of Jesus' suffering and death. This radically redefines the common image of God.[8] For the Christian, God is no longer the monarch

---

8. A highly influential work on this subject is *The Crucified God* by Jürgen Moltmann,

who rules from above, but the God who is present in the life and ministry of Jesus, submitting with him to the humiliation and suffering of the cross. In identifying God with the life and mission of Jesus, his suffering takes on redemptive power; the cross becomes a symbol of the love and compassion of God who suffers with us even unto death.

The good news that Jesus embodies and that the cross symbolizes is that God is compassionate and forgiving, that God actually seeks out those who have lost their way (Luke 15), and that salvation is found in his embrace. It is at this individual level that the meaning of the cross is found. The metaphysical big picture created in transactional atonement theories is at best irrelevant to that happening, and can even pose a harmful distraction. Escaping judgment is dubious motivation for arriving at faith, but the big picture in most atonement theories has certainly made its contribution to the attempt.

Lifting up the individual before God as the context for salvation does not mean that there is no cosmic dimension to "being saved." The God of redemption cannot be divorced from the God of creation, which introduces quite a different big picture from those we've been discussing. It is not a theory, but the expression of Christian hope. It does not limit salvation but expands the concept to include all of creation. Paul uses a striking metaphor in speaking of creation as "groaning in travail" with us (Rom 8:22–23), awaiting the consummation. The Bible thinks big when it comes to that future in which God will be "all in all." The great transformation it envisions will bring a new heaven and a new earth, a concept that defies our imagination but clearly signals an all-encompassing metamorphosis that will liberate our world from the bondage of death and decay. Our lives are entwined with the whole of God's creation, and whatever our destiny, it is one which we share together. From this conviction it should be obvious that we are responsible for the creation that nourishes and sustains us. Whatever form taken by an ultimate transformation, one truth we can infer is that "we are all in this together."

Heaven and Hell

Rooted in historical events and bearing the promise of the gospel, Christian faith quite naturally moves from past, to present, to future, envisioning a

---

which appeared in English translation in 1973. A fortieth anniversary edition has recently appeared.

consummation to the story of humanity and humanity's world. A prominent biblical theme in this eschatological faith is that we are accountable for the life we have led. Jesus pictures a "last judgment" (Matt 25:31–46) in which the messianic figure, the Son of Man, whom we identify with Jesus, comes in all of his glory. He is accompanied by angels and sits on his throne, judging the Gentile nations that are assembled before him. He pictures our response to those in various kinds of need—the hungry, the sick, the imprisoned—as a response to Jesus himself. His picturing this scene is his way of framing the human story, driving home the ultimate importance of his ethic for all people, that we love God and love our neighbor. The sense of ultimacy is enhanced by his picturing the consequence of our actions, where those fulfilling the command to love enter "eternal life," and those failing to love being sent to "eternal punishment."

From ancient times, the church has treated this story as a literal description of what is going to happen at the end of history as we know it, with judgment resulting in one's entry either into heaven or hell. Is this an interpretation that we can appropriately make today? The idea that heaven and hell are *places*—geographical locations—has exercised the pious imagination of believers throughout the ages, but today these "places of destination" are more likely subjects for comedians and the comic strips. The pearly gates and streets of gold, as well as the fires of hell and the wiles of the devil, have long ago been transferred to the realm of symbol and metaphor, but even then their value as theological images can be questioned.

The Bible contains a fair amount of apocalyptic material, picturing in highly imaginative fashion the outcome of history in terms of judgment, condemnation, and reward. Rather than literalizing an imaginary picture as presented in Matthew 25, we should discern the meaning. I believe an appropriate interpretation is that we recognize the universal imperative to live our lives with a spirit of compassion. Without regard to class, status, religious affiliation, or any other distinction, we are all claimed by the imperative to love our neighbor, particularly the neighbor in need. The life of compassion is a universal expectation of the God of compassion, and any thinking on the part of Christians about a future consummation should be governed by that God of the gospel whom we know in Christ.

We bring to bear this gospel perspective when we stop defining judgment as condemnation. Retributive judgment may well play a role in civil government, but when it comes to the gospel of Jesus Christ, judgment takes on a quite different character. It is judgment that glorifies the God we call Father, whose justice is tempered by mercy, whose righteousness is the source of our redemption.

> God's judgment is far higher and better than [retribution]; it involves "putting things right." It means reconciling and restoring, not merely punishing; healing, not merely diagnosing; transforming, not merely exposing; revaluing (or redeeming), not merely evaluating ... in the end God will be all in all, and all shall be well, and all manner of things shall be well.[9]

As people of faith we affirm that God is sovereign over both life and death, both present and future, but what shape and form the future will take is beyond the powers of imagination. The New Testament emphasis lies on something utterly new, on transformation, as we saw in the resurrection of Jesus. The Apostle Paul imagines the sound of a trumpet, calling forth the dead to a new, transfigured life. What we see in that language is not a description of final events, but faith in God who will make all things new. I would lift up the words in the First Letter of John, who unites our future with the risen Christ: "Beloved, we are God's children now; it does not yet appear what we shall be, but we know that when he appears we shall be like him, for we shall see him as he is" (1 John 3:2). This is John's way of saying that the resurrection hope will be fulfilled in us, but what that means we simply do not know. The essential meaning for believers is that we can live and die with a faith that puts all things into the hands of a loving God.

---

9. McLaren, *A New Kind of Christianity*, 204–5.

Chapter Ten

New Directions in the Life of the Church

We are in a time of transition, and that transition is not a casual or passing one. Rather, it is yet another of the semi-millennial upheavals that have shaped latinized [western] culture and religion from their inception. We are citizens living within the Great Emergence, and as Christians of whatever stripe, we are watching the formation of a new presentation of the faith. We are attending upon the birth and early growth of Emergence Christianity.

—Phyllis Tickle[1]

If the cluster of images that we call Christ is to be compelling in the postmodern age, it will be in the context of the particular historical community, the Church, that lives out of that heritage. To affirm the contemporaneity of Christ is to affirm the viability of the Church in at least some one of its lines of development . . . . [U]nless there is some viable community, the image of Christ will become so diffuse that it will not have significant directing power.

—William A. Beardslee[2]

---

1. Tickle, *Emergence Christianity*, 28.
2. See Beardslee, "Christ in the Postmodern Age," 78.

Christian Faith in Our Time

In this effort at rethinking the church's theology, my focus has been on the present, postmodern age. This is understandable, since the transition from modernity to postmodernity has created many of the issues that compel our attention today in rethinking doctrines of the faith. But there is value in taking a broader view of history in order to better comprehend the dimensions of our present situation. In this chapter I turn to the church in our time, a subject that invites taking a broader historical view to help us recognize the significance of what we are experiencing today.

Emergence Christianity

Phyllis Tickle has been a prominent writer in chronicling religious change in western history. The founding editor of the religion department of *Publishers Weekly* and a former academic, she is the author of some two dozen books on religion in America.[3] Tickle discerns periodic "tsunamis" in the history of Christianity, great upheavals occurring roughly every 500 years and bringing momentous change to the course of Christian history. Following the birth of Christianity 2,000 years ago, there came "the Great Transformation" some 500 years later with the decline and fall of the Roman Empire and the subsequent Dark Ages, when monastic Christianity emerged as the defining expression of the church. Then came "the Great Schism" in the eleventh century between East and West, creating a permanent division between two estranged churches and two opposing cultures. The third upheaval in the sixteenth century was "the Great Reformation," with the emergence of Protestantism and the radical reshaping of western Christianity. With religion deeply embedded in the life of the people, most of these transitions brought momentous change to the larger cultural, economic, and political scene.

The thesis of Tickle and other observers is that now, some 500 years after the Reformation, we are in the midst of the fourth transitional phase whose outcome is not yet discernible. Various terms have been used to describe this current transition, including "the Great Mutation," and "the Great Convergence," but the favored term seems to be "the Great Emergence." It signals the arrival of a new Christian consciousness that is affecting the whole church, but most obviously the conservative, evangelical churches for whom the times are bringing dramatic changes. Among other

---

3. Two works of Phyllis Tickle that are particularly germane to the evolving scene are *The Great Emergence* and *Emergence Christianity*.

things, evangelicals are being challenged to rethink the way in which they interpret and communicate the gospel message, and what their stance should be in relation to other religious traditions. Emergence Christianity is a distinctively postmodern phenomenon, reflecting much of the thinking and attitude that has led to my own attempt to rethink the church's theology. A concrete expression today of Emergence Christianity is the so-called "emergent church."

The Emergent Church

The emergent church began to form during the decade of the 1990s. The leaders of the movement for the most part were raised in conservative evangelical churches, including a significant number of pastors engaged in youth ministry. Tony Jones, a prominent figure in the movement, sees three characteristics in emergent Christians: 1) they are largely people who are greatly disappointed with modern American Christianity, with the way the gospel has been presented to them, and the way it has been lived in the contemporary church; 2) they are people with a pronounced desire for inclusion, including openness and a nonjudgmental spirit, but not necessarily being identified as liberal or progressive in their Christian beliefs; and 3) they are people with a "hope-filled orientation," focusing on the good news of the gospel both now and on Judgment Day, and partnering with God in building the kingdom of God in contemporary society.[4]

Emergent Christians want to move beyond the liberal vs. conservative polarity that has dominated political and religious life in the modern period. They are critical of both mainline and evangelical churches where they have bought into ideologies of "left" and "right"; they seek a postmodern path that identifies Christianity in terms of a faithful life that takes precedence over theological beliefs. For "emergents," as they are called, community and relationships are at the center of Christian life, and the church they have fashioned reflects this conviction. It is not the building that is the church, but Christians who gather for worship and fellowship. Thus the site for such gatherings may be a coffee shop, a home, or the basement of a rented church. Gathering usually in small numbers, the atmosphere is casual; fellowship is encouraged by sitting on soft furniture around tables rather than rows of pews. The sermon is typically marked by interaction and can lead to extended discussion. Membership rolls are not generally

4. Jones, *The New Christians*, 70–72.

maintained. Emergents are highly suspicious of the hierarchy and bureaucracy that they see in the established churches, emphasizing the virtues of a decentralized church and focusing on the local congregation as the center of Christian life.

A particularly significant postmodern characteristic of emergent Christians is what Jones calls their "epistemic humility" (from the Greek word "to know"), a theme shared by this book. Emergents generally have been alienated by the overconfident dogmatism of conservative churches, claiming for themselves an absolute truth that places everyone else under judgment. A pluralistic world not only contradicts this kind of attitude, but in a positive way compels Christians to recognize the heart and soul of the church's message: the good news of the grace, love, and mercy of God. Epistemic humility (or modesty) encourages a respectful stance toward those in other religious traditions, to say nothing of those within one's own tradition with whom one disagrees. Respect and dialogue are principal features of the emergent mentality in addressing theological differences. Rather than using them as an occasion to draw lines in the sand, theological disagreements call for continuing conversation.[5]

Brian McLaren is a pastor, theologian, and activist in the emergent church who has been particularly influential. A former college English professor, McLaren has been called "the Martin Luther of Emergence Christianity." He would rather describe his role as one who is "reformulating" the church's tradition rather than reforming it. In any event, he has been a lightning rod for much criticism coming from conservative evangelicals. The publication of one of McLaren's books[6] precipitated a crisis in the early stages of the emerging church. Conservative evangelicals in the movement took exception to his theology and went their separate way. The terms "emerging" and "emergent" were being used interchangeably up to that time, but now the conservative faction was called the emerging church, and the more progressive faction the emergent church, two groupings within

---

5. The doctrinal statement of an emergent community in New York simply reads, "We commit to ongoing discussion, as a Community, of our understanding of Scripture and contemporary life in the light of holy Tradition. We commit ourselves to the best use of Reason of which we are capable in all our reading, learning, and discussion."

6. McLaren, *A New Kind of Christian*. The book features a dialogue between a burned-out evangelical preacher and a high school science teacher who had been a Presbyterian pastor. The preacher laments that he is losing "the whole framework for my faith," and the teacher responds, "You have a modern faith, a faith that you developed in your homeland of modernity. But you're immigrating into a new land, a postmodern world" (12, 13).

New Directions in the Life of the Church

Emergence Christianity. This rupture has been a painful reminder of the tenacity of perennial theological divisions within the church, but it also testifies to the innovative and bold thinking of McLaren.

The desire of emergents to move beyond the antinomies common to theology in the modern age is engagingly stated in the subtitle of McLaren's book, *A Generous Orthodoxy: Why I am a missional, evangelical, post/protestant, liberal/conservative, mystical/poetic, biblical, charismatic/ contemplative, fundamentalist/calvinist, anabaptist/anglican, methodist, catholic, green, incarnational, depressed-yet-hopeful, emergent, unfinished CHRISTIAN.*[7] The resolve of emergents not to be typed one way or another—being "put in a box"—accounts for their refusal to issue a confessional statement, reflecting, too, their conviction that the crux of Christian faith is not found in particular beliefs but in the life that faith inspires. This stance has predictably drawn fire from conservatives who complain that emergents are "slippery" and "squishy," failing to take a stand.

This raises a disturbing fact. The emergent church is lifting up the ideals of moderation and inclusiveness, with a corresponding rejection of dogmatism in theology and the exclusive spirit that it generates. The fact is, however, that moderation and openness tend to be strangers to the religious temperament; the consequences inherent to religious belief are perceived to be so serious that there is really no alternative to the attitude of either/or—you either believe or you don't, and you'd better know just where you stand. Certainty and confidence are typically identified with a strong religious life, and that life is enhanced by strict doctrines and moral codes that clearly distinguish the believer from the non-believer. The growth of conservative evangelical churches in recent decades, while mainline churches were losing members, has been cited as proof that people seek the security bestowed by an authoritarian church. All of which suggests that the emergent church has embarked on an uphill course.

Nonetheless, I believe that today's church must encourage an attitude of openness and acceptance toward the "other," whatever the beliefs or lack of beliefs that one finds there. A new orientation toward the pluralistic world is called for, moving away from the defensiveness and judgmental spirit that too often has characterized the church. This should not signal a minimizing of belief or willingness to compromise on essentials of one's faith. What it does signal is greater maturity of faith, a recognition that deep conviction does not require a spirit of dogmatism or defensiveness,

---

7. McLaren, *A Generous Orthodoxy*.

which are marks of insecurity and weakness rather than strength. It signals the willingness to live by the spirit of Christ, recognizing that there is no more powerful witness to divine truth than to walk in the way of compassion and respect.

We might put it this way: the shrunken world of the postmodern era—what we often refer to as the "global village"—calls for a new orientation on the part of Christians. We are no longer gatekeepers on behalf of God, a role we have readily played in the past when we could comfortably identify with an imperial church that possessed the keys to the kingdom. That kind of thinking identifies salvation with "getting to heaven" rather than being made whole, being spiritually restored and healed. We are gradually moving away from that way of thinking but much too slowly; it requires more explicit intention on the part of the church to refrain from identifying the consequences of religious belief with one's eternal destiny, either heaven or hell. Our belief in resurrection bestows the conviction that God is Lord over our death as well as our life, and that is enough. It does not permit us to hold forth on the eternal destiny of believers and non-believers, which is not only speculation but intolerable pride. God alone knows the hearts of his creatures.

Another quote from Tony Jones gives evidence of postmodern themes in Emergence Christianity that also enter into my own rethinking of theology:

> . . . the Christian gospel is always enculturated, always articulated by a certain people in a certain time and place. To try to freeze one particular articulation of the gospel, to make it timeless and universally applicable, actually does an injustice to the gospel. This goes to the very heart of what emergent is and of how emergent Christians are attempting to chart a course for following Jesus in the postmodern, globalized, pluralized world of the twenty-first century.[8]

Together with this sensibility of a changing world, emergents bring a healthy sense of the Christian tradition; their purpose is not to abandon ancient truths, but to reassess and reinterpret those truths in a postmodern setting. This willingness to engage the tradition actually sharpens their ability to articulate just what the church's gospel is all about. For many, their early experience of Christianity has been constrictive and stifling, which gives added impetus to their desire for a more generous understanding of

---

8. Jones, *The New Christians*, 96.

New Directions in the Life of the Church

the faith. They see themselves as agents of change, defining what it means to be Christians in a postmodern world.

The reach of Emergence Christianity goes well beyond North America. It is a worldwide phenomenon, powered by the advent of cyberspace and the Internet. Emergents live in daily connection with their friends around the globe, contributing to their spirit of ecumenism. While growth of the movement is desirable, they resist the idea that success for the church is measured in numbers—a "capitalist" notion. Rather, sustainability is the goal for each congregation, whether it numbers in the tens or hundreds. Thus emergents do not see themselves as competing with established denominations; they are not out to proselytize. The term "Hyphenateds" has been applied to those members of other churches who will often attend emergent worship services but who choose to remain in their own church.

Phyllis Tickle notes the unique backgrounds in Emergence Christianity, with close to one quarter of emergent Christians tracing their roots to Azusa, California where Pentecostalism received a rebirth in American Christianity. In addition, a significant number of reform-minded emergents, coming from mainline churches, find their inspiration in the social gospel movement initiated by the ministry of Walter Rauschenbusch in the early twentieth century. This mixture of a Spirit piety with a commitment to social justice contributes to the uniqueness of the emergent church. Its awareness of postmodern sensibilities also contributes to the effectiveness of its message and presence.

Not surprisingly, emergents are facing a literal barrage of irate commentary from fundamentalists and many evangelicals who regard them as a renegade church, people of their own flock who have forsaken the true faith. The break with fundamentalism is, in fact, a defining feature of the emergent church that holds particular promise. Evangelical churches have long labored under the burden of a fundamentalist understanding of Scripture, which today is widely recognized as obscurantist. Ironically, in its own twisted way the fundamentalist view of Scripture is quite rational, judging the Bible's truth and validity on the basis of its (scientific) factuality. If a biblical story did not actually happen—if it is not *literally* true—then it has no truth value for the believer. This way of hearing the Bible's message is stone deaf to the variety of ways in which biblical language assumes a revelatory power in addressing the human situation. It also reflects the unwillingness of fundamentalists and many conservatives to engage in the historical and literary work that is critical to understanding the biblical message.

The emergent emphasis on a generous orthodoxy is helpful and contagious, both affirming the church's tradition and challenging the assumptions that can turn that tradition into a wooden set of dogmatic answers. However, what its impact might be in the long run does face some significant issues. One obvious question is how long a decentralized, non-bureaucratic church can survive. Its congregational polity, which identifies the church exclusively with the local congregation, also raises the question whether the emergent commitment to social justice and peace can exert a significant impact on society; that would seem to require a strong national organization. But whatever their future, emergent Christians clearly have a role to play in today's church, and we would hope a role of renewal and reform.

While emergence Christianity is broadly seen as a movement emerging from conservative, evangelical Christianity, it is actually a broader phenomenon that involves mainline churches as well. In that context, it tends not to be regarded as a theological movement, creating waves because of a more generous orthodoxy. That is because mainline churches have already been moving in the direction of a more generous orthodoxy, unevenly and incrementally as it may be. The focus, rather, is on a more effective outreach to the unchurched, with methods of the emergent church being replicated.

My own church offers an example of this development. Under the leadership of its director for new congregations, the Evangelical Lutheran Church in America has begun an impressive number of worshiping communities in a variety of settings, including homes, bars, train stations, and other locations on the streets. The church is seen as the gathering of neighbors where they are, with a particular desire to connect with the working poor and young adults. The ELCA is basically a church of transplanted Scandinavians and Germans, but these new communities are quite diverse, with 56 percent of them being led by people of color.[9] Initiatives of this kind bear considerable promise in broadening the horizons of the church and invigorating its commitment to spreading the gospel message.

Changing the Church's Priorities

The decline of religion in this postmodern age has been an ongoing topic for pollsters and commentators, particularly in recent years. Polling statistics as well as declining church attendance indicate a steady weakening

---

9. Merritt, "Shut up and learn."

of loyalty to all forms of organized religion. The fastest growing religious demographic are the "nones," those who do not claim membership in a religious organization. One can assume that many if not most nones are lapsed Christians who for one reason or another have been alienated by the church, or who have simply concluded that the church is irrelevant to their lives. It may well be that many of the drop-outs, those whom the Episcopal bishop John Spong has ironically referred to as "the church's alumni association," have never been committed members of the church in the first place; their departure has been encouraged by what they perceive in societal attitudes about the church.

For whatever reasons, the exodus of church members is a significant event and a matter of justified concern among Christians. This is not because numbers are the standard for evaluating the church or for assessing the truth of its message. Indeed, one might argue (as did the Danish philosopher Søren Kierkegaard) that a significant reformation within the church would likely result in the exodus of vast numbers of people whose commitment to the way of Christ is nominal or lukewarm at best. A smaller church would likely be a more faithful church. And yet, such thinking has always posed a dilemma because the church is fundamentally inclusive, not exclusive. It cannot operate as a highly disciplined task force, with a required set of beliefs and a clear blueprint for social action. The church by its very nature is open to all, with a deep sense of divine grace and acceptance as the bedrock of the church's life together. Living with this tension created by the gospel as both gift and task, grace and discipleship, characterizes the life of the church. Striking a proper balance between these poles is the mark of a faithful Christian community.

The emergent church is correct in seeing the critical need of a stronger sense of community within the church. Its emphasis on relationships gets to the core of what the church is about. That sensibility is expressed by Diana Butler Bass in what she terms "the Great Reversal," in which she reverses the order of priorities established by the Reformation.[10] That Reformation order can be expressed in the three words: "believing, behavior, belonging." The first word establishes the priority of theology, or getting the beliefs right in one's head. The second word sees behavior as the result of belief—right belief leads to right behavior. The third word, "belonging," places community as the end result, or dependent upon, right believing and behavior.

10. Bass, *Christianity after Religion*, 204.

Bass proposes the opposite order as appropriate to the emerging Christian consciousness and a more vital church: "belonging, behavior, believing." Christianity is community above all with its sense of belonging, a new life together created by the encounter with the living Christ. That experience creates a distinctive spirituality with its attendant behavior, the community now seeking to live "in Christ." Lastly, the community seeks to express its new life in appropriate propositions or statements of belief. This order reflects the postmodern outlook that prioritizes experience over reason and propositional truth. Bass claims that it is an order that first characterized Christianity but which was reversed as a result of the Reformation. It needs to be recovered for the sake of a renewed and inclusive church.

One sees a similar disenchantment with traditional western theology in the work of theologian Harvey Cox, who wants to recapture the "movement" character of Christianity that he identifies with its first three centuries. A momentous turn in the history of Christianity took place in the fourth century when it became an imperial religion under Emperor Constantine. That change, says Cox, initiated the deterioration of Christianity "from a movement generated by faith and hope into a religious empire demarcated by prescribed doctrines and ruled by a priestly elite." In effect, faith in Christ was turned into belief in the correctness of theological statements *about* Christ. In our time Cox sees the potential of a rebirth of Christianity in which its vital centers are becoming worldwide, including Asia, Africa, and Latin America, where liberation theology conveys a more authentic grasp of Jesus' teaching of the kingdom of God. It generates a this-worldly spirituality, centering on justice and liberation of the oppressed.[11]

My rethinking the church's theology brings an additional dimension to this subject, recognizing the metaphorical nature of theological language and its accent upon the Mystery that is God. It means that theology cannot bear the kind of weight that it has in the past. *Theology does not bring a life-or-death character to the fundamental propositions of faith; it does not draw the lines that divide the saved from the lost, which in the past has been the nature of Christian belief.* Without doubt that understanding has contributed significantly to the church's prioritizing of belief. If *what* you believe makes the critical difference in your eternal destiny, the importance of theology becomes *absolute, final.* We need to establish a different orientation in which theology is truly the servant of the life of faith rather than the standard bearer of eternal judgment. That should enable a more single-minded

---

11. Cox, *The Future of Faith*, 55–56.

concentration on the good news of the gospel revealed in Jesus Christ, and the life of faith that it inspires. As far as judgment is concerned, this reorientation will focus it primarily on one's own lack of faith and failure to live a fruitful life of discipleship. This is self-judgment, the capacity for which is an essential ingredient of a mature faith.

Chapter Eleven

Challenges to Church and Faith

Christianity finds itself in a quite new situation in relation to other religions ... Christians are now open to serious dialogue.... [W]ithin all religions there are now those who recognize that the moment has come to engage seriously in an effort not only to understand each other but also, through that, to understand themselves better.

—Jerald Brauer[1]

Doubt has been viewed as a threat to faith when in fact it is the absence of doubt that corrodes and destroys both human reason and faith. Faith without doubt is less a form of faithfulness and more a form of blindness. Faith in dialogue with doubt, however, offers a way of understanding the limits of both reason and faith. Reason cannot explain all, just as faith cannot explain all.... The inexplicable, that which resists understanding, is at the heart of everything.

—Guy Collins[2]

---

1. Brauer, "A New Paradigm for Theology?" 208.
2. Collins, *Faithful Doubt*, 50–51.

Challenges to Church and Faith

In concluding this work with two chapters on the church I want to acknowledge the indispensability of the church to Christian faith. Christians are individuals, but as Christians they are part of a community of faith that bestows their identity as followers of Christ. Theology is important to the Christian's self-identity, but the worshiping community is the lifeblood of the Christian. This fact makes a painful scandal of the many divisions within the church, dating back to the sixteenth-century Reformation. Those divisions have been all the more scandalous because of the painful acrimony and hostility that has often characterized their relationships. In recent times—often referred to as "the ecumenical age"—these ruptures appear to be healing, and one of the welcome features of the emergent church is its explicit commitment to that healing process. Its statement on this matter deserves to be quoted:

> We are committed to honor and serve the church in all its forms—Orthodox, Roman Catholic, Protestant, Pentecostal, Anabaptist. We practice "deep ecclesiology"—rather than favoring some forms of the church and critiquing or rejecting others, we see that every form of the church has both weaknesses and strengths, both liabilities and potential . . . We own the many failures of the church as our failures, which humbles us and calls us to repentance, and we also celebrate the many heroes and virtues of the church, which inspires us and gives us hope.[3]

In terms of organization the church may never be completely united, nor should that be expected. What is needed is a spirit of respect and understanding between the churches, where each church respects the distinctive history and heritage of the others. It also requires the kind of mind-set encouraged by the rethinking of theology, where differences in theological positions can be accepted or at least understood in light of the historical contexts that produced them. This kind of generous orthodoxy exalts the unity of the church that underlies all of its differences. Recognizing and celebrating that unity is urgently needed today, not only for the sake of the church's integrity but for the sake of its witness in the world. In this closing chapter I want to note several challenges the church faces to its life and witness in the postmodern culture.

---

3. Jones, *The New Christians*, appendix A, 223–24.

Spirituality versus Religion?

One might conclude that the decline of the church is evidence of a growing secularism in society, but that appears to oversimplify what is happening. It may reflect more of a disaffection with institutional religion, a postmodern suspicion of bureaucracy and tradition that we noticed in the attitude of emergent Christians. The decline of organized religion in the postmodern era has, in fact, been accompanied by an intense interest in personal spirituality. This development centers on the individual rather than the community, with spiritual practices designed to foster a more satisfying life, one that promises greater personal fulfillment.

I believe that underlying the spirituality phenomenon is the desire to find a conclusive meaning or purpose in life, beyond pursuing material satisfactions or a superficial happiness. The spiritual person seeks an integrated life in the face of daily distractions, moving beyond a fragmented existence to a sense of wholeness. It involves the search for a deeper level of meaning and dedicating oneself to finding it and realizing it within oneself. All of this may include acknowledgment of a "higher power," or it may not. The wonders of nature and the mystery of the universe, for example, can evoke a spiritual attitude without reference to God. In any event, the individual is typically charting the course in this quest rather than an authoritative community or institution.

The individualism that dominates the American psyche has proven to be fertile soil for the growth of spirituality. It has also nurtured a consumer attitude in which the individual picks and chooses what best serves his or her interests. This gives spirituality an eclectic character where one is open to whatever is personally appealing. The spiritual person may be informed by books and gurus representing a variety of traditions, from Buddhism to Hinduism, from Christianity to humanism, without much concern with contradictions or inconsistencies between them. This reflects a postmodern emphasis upon experience rather than rationality, with a corresponding lack of interest in theology as the rational attempt to formulate and understand one's beliefs. And of course, where it's a purely individual spirituality there is no institutional authority that could call one to account for an inadequate spirituality.

While one can appreciate the desire for wholeness and integration that spirituality conveys, it is disconcerting to see how it is often used as a means for other ends. Entrepreneurs in the business world are using the interest in spirituality as a means of enhancing the atmosphere in the workplace and improving the performance of their employees, all for the goal of a more profitable business. Fitness centers and health care facilities also feature spirituality courses as a come-on for prospective clients. In this setting the practice of spirituality is dominated by techniques and methods that would guarantee success in achieving a more satisfying spiritual life. If the quest for a deepened spirituality is not resolutely pursued as an end in itself, as it is in the context of religious belief, it too easily succumbs to the pressures of a consumer society that will turn it into a routine that has lost its spiritual meaning.

The individual-centered spirituality of our time has led some commentators to conclude that we are witnessing a cultural transition from religion to spirituality, from tradition-based, community-centered faith to individual beliefs and spiritual practices. This viewpoint typically portrays institutional religion in very jaundiced terms: it is doctrinaire, authoritarian, moralistic, legalistic, and hierarchical, with too much attention given to buildings and raising money. This kind of critique can border on caricature, failing to recognize that at the heart of every religion is a spiritual vision that gives it substance and depth. As we have noted, spirituality divorced from religious traditions is vulnerable to misuse, including also the inclination to give it a self-centered interpretation that fails to motivate the individual to a larger vision of the common good. A helpful analogy has been offered on this subject: religion is to spirituality as institutions of learning are to education.

Rather than regarding individual spirituality as a sequel to religion, in effect replacing religion, its presence today as a distinctive feature of postmodern culture should be seen as a challenge and opportunity for the church. For one thing, it should encourage congregations to focus more deeply on Christian spirituality and practices that nurture one's faith. In chapter 4 we noted several dimensions of faith, including primarily "trust" and "faithfulness." These two terms aptly describe the spirituality of Christians, placing them in relationship to the God they know in Christ Jesus. Christian spirituality is living in relationship, related to God in a spirit of trust and devotion, and to one's neighbor in a spirit of love and respect. There is no more powerful depiction of what this means than in the teaching of Jesus. His parable of the Prodigal Son depicts God as the merciful, compassionate father who embraces his lost son, inspiring trust and devotion. And his parable of the Good Samaritan depicts the faithful life to which we are called, reaching out in love and compassion to the one in need, even if a stranger or an enemy.

In other words, Christian spirituality is much more than pursuing a fulfilling experience. It is a way of life that is best characterized as a calling, a vocation to bring a spirit of neighbor-love to all of one's relationships. Christian spirituality identifies faith with faithfulness, with discipleship, with moral sensitivity and responsibility. *Faith is nourished by prayer and worship, and is expressed in the compassionate life.* This is where the example of Jesus plays such a decisive and powerful role. His cruciform life beckons every Christian to live a self-giving life, one that recognizes the healing balm of a life that is willing to give to the point of sacrifice. It is a life that seeks to embrace the neighbor both near and far, that is sensitive to the injustice in the world and the pain and agony it creates for so many of God's creatures. Christian spirituality is no individual matter, nor limited to the cultivation of spiritual practices. It issues in a Christ-centered life.

The obvious advantage in being part of a religious community is that it provides resources and support for one's spiritual growth. The church as a community of faith is an essential component of the Christian's spirituality, holding up the vision of an authentic life of discipleship. But ultimately spirituality is an individual matter, involving a willingness to exercise the discipline needed to live in the spirit of Christ. It is significant that the words "disciple" and "discipline" are derived from the same Latin word. To be a follower of Christ requires self-discipline.

The Church among World Religions

The Greek language has two words for time, *chronos* and *kairos*. The former refers to the passing of time, from days to months to years. The latter refers to time in the sense of "the right time," or "the opportune moment." In the New Testament *kairos* receives a theological meaning, referring to "the fullness of time" or God's appointed time in which a divine purpose is being fulfilled. I believe Christians should see our present time as a *kairos* moment on a worldwide scale, a time of momentous change in which the church is being challenged to respond to a radically new situation in its relation to other religious traditions. It is a situation that carries tremendous possibilities in fostering positive relationships among the world religions, and without question the response of Christians to this challenge will have a decisive impact in making it happen.

A modest theology recognizes this truth, bringing a spirit of hospitality in relating Christian faith to other religions of the world. By this I mean that Christians are called to exemplify a spirit of openness and acceptance in their relations with members of other religious traditions. *This attitude should be a prominent part of Christian spirituality and an essential feature of the image projected by the church.* Among other things, it demonstrates respect for the other, taking seriously the ethic generated by the gospel. It also indicates that we are willing to recognize that we can be blessed by the insights of other traditions, which means that we can profit from entering into dialogue with those of other faiths.

Traditionalists will complain that this attitude implies that Christian faith is inadequate or insufficient, needing help from other religious traditions. That is a defensive reaction typical of the modern period. Openness to dialogue means that our faith is willing to recognize and acknowledge that the Spirit of God is moving in the hearts and lives of those who do not share our history and tradition. It means that we are willing to forsake the notion that the truth that we confess does not allow for truth to be found in other religions of the world. It means that we are willing to recognize that we can profit from listening to and reflecting on the spiritual insights of other traditions.

Unfortunately, there is much that stands in the way of adopting this hospitable view. An all-too-common fact about Christian attitudes toward other religions is that the stronger one's faith, or at least the more pronounced one's loyalty to the church, the more likely that suspicion and even hostility will mark one's attitude toward other religions. The implication would seem to be that if a strong faith makes one hostile, then it takes a weak or lukewarm faith for one to be accepting of other religions. But isn't there a third alternative? Brian McLaren poses the critical question:

> Shouldn't it be possible to have a strong Christian identity that is strongly benevolent toward people of other faiths, accepting them not *in spite of* the religion they love, but *with* the religion they love? Could my love and respect for them as human beings lead me to a loving and respectful encounter with their religion as well?[4]

The world in which we are now living clearly compels Christians to find this third alternative, and given the proliferation of interreligious dialogues and books that commend interreligious understanding, that quest is well

---

4. McLaren, *Why Did Jesus, Moses, the Buddha, and Mohammed Cross the Road?*, 32.

underway. But it is not simply a matter of being coerced by the times in which we live; it is rather a question of Christian identity, of who we are as Christians. If we are to be true to ourselves, we will extend the hand of hospitality to those of other religious traditions.

One typical response to this issue is to raise the flag of evangelism. As I was recently told by a friend and fellow church member, the only acceptable response to those of other religions is to "convert them." He didn't say what his response would be if they failed to convert, but there is enough history concerning interfaith relations to guarantee that it would likely be ugly. Humans tend to identify themselves by the groups to which they belong, and when one's group is challenged or thwarted by a competing group, the situation easily erupts into violence. When it comes to religious groups, unfortunately, the tensions are magnified. The stakes then are perceived to be one's eternal destiny, and it doesn't get more serious than that. Religious warfare has typically been the most fanatical and violent that humanity has known.

Christians will appeal to Scripture in supporting their views on this subject, but because the New Testament does not specifically address the situation we now face, one finds a verse that can be interpreted in a way that supports one's position. Probably more than any one verse in the Bible, John 14:6 has been used to justify the notion that salvation is limited to those who believe in Jesus Christ: "Jesus said to [Thomas], 'I am the way, and the truth, and the life. No one comes to the Father except through me.'" A responsible exegesis of this passage would first note its context. Jesus is in the Upper Room with his disciples, sharing a final meal before his execution. He tells them that he will soon depart "to prepare a place for you," and that they "know the way" to where he is going. Thomas takes exception to this statement, saying that the disciples don't know where he is going and thus do not know the way. Jesus then responds that he is "the way, the truth, and the life."

Jesus is not responding to the question whether there are other paths to God in addition to him, as though he were competing with the Buddha or the future Muhammad. He is addressing his disciples in a moment of great stress, and wants to assure them that they have seen in him the way to God the Father. He assures them that they need not seek another way than what they know in him. He emphasizes that point in order to comfort and strengthen them; they are not being forsaken. His words include an implicit exhortation: "Continue in the way that you have come to know in me; be faithful disciples." What we hear in John 14:6 is a word to all of Jesus' followers to be faithful in their commitment to Jesus, and to be confident in entrusting themselves to him.

The misinterpretation of this verse in the history of the church has been not only ironic in light of its proper understanding, but a great tragedy when one considers the consequences it has inspired. Its use as a means of exalting Christianity as the exclusive avenue to God has justified all kinds of violence perpetrated against people who have been perceived as enemies of the gospel—and all in the name of Jesus! The church has much to repent of, and in mending its ways it must recognize and clearly proclaim that Jesus Christ transcends the church and the Christian religion. We do not possess Jesus, and cannot use him or our relation to him to justify the denigrating and judgment of other religious groups. The most common form of that practice is to claim salvation as an exclusive possession of the church.

As we've noted, the emphasis on theology in the wake of the Reformation has accentuated the differences between Christian churches, and that outlook has had the same impact on Christianity's relation to other religions. Throughout the modern period, the assumption of an exclusive truth that we possess as Christians has led to the conclusion that all other religions had to be false. This frame of mind is now changing; instead of theology as the standard for religious truth, postmodern theologians point to the faithful life as the ultimate measure of religious truth. This promising move gives weight to the adage, "by their fruits you shall know them." At the same time one has to acknowledge that whether it is theology or the faithful life that serves as the standard of faith, the threat of legalism hovers close by. The seriousness of the religious mind and temperament must be infused with a deep consciousness that in all things we live by grace.

Theology is essential to the extent that it contributes to the life of faith, clarifying and nurturing the Christian life, but it can also function as a dogmatic battering ram when it succumbs to the rational quest for certainty and security. A dogmatic attitude will always secure itself at the expense of the other. Now is the time to recognize that our allegiance to Jesus beckons us to a hospitable and potentially fruitful relationship with those who have been nourished by a different religious tradition. It does not mean that we are required to remove our differences, or to ignore them. But we can and ought to celebrate what we find in common—likely much more than we might anticipate.

If we truly believe that "God is love" (1 John 4:16), and that God would have everyone enter into a saving relationship with God (1 Tim 2:4), then as Christians we must put behind us the barriers of exclusivism that have dominated our past. The Spirit of God, whom we know in Jesus, is the Spirit of love that we cannot direct or control. The Spirit "moves where it will," bringing God's presence into every heart that is moved beyond its self-centered fears and desires. If a fruitful Christian experience truly conveys this encounter with God, then we can expect to see similar fruits in the lives of those whose divine encounter takes place apart from the Christian witness and ethos. Such fruits would include a sense of divine grace, a spirit of gratitude and devotion, the gifts of the Spirit that Paul describes in Galatians 5:22–25; in effect, a reorientation of one's life. To deny the presence of such gifts beyond the Christian context is not only to close one's eyes but to deny the presence of the Spirit throughout human life and experience.[5]

For many Christians today, the plea on behalf of hospitality rings hollow or at least appears dubious because of the emergence of radical Islam. Given today's circumstances, isn't hospitality a dead end, an invitation to "give up the ship"? I would say that on the contrary, today's circumstances compel us all the more to demonstrate genuine hospitality to the Muslim community, which in many ways is more vulnerable to the threat of Muslim extremists than are the rest of us. Our acceptance of the Muslim today assumes particular importance and meaning because it demonstrates that the most extreme challenges will not lead us to forsake our Christian calling as peacemakers. To do so would only deepen the conflict and invite the Armageddon that extremists on both sides would like to see happen. Limited military action on the part of the international community may well be necessary in this conflict, but the Christian community must be attentive to its possible long-term consequences and contribute to the growing of peaceful relationships at the grassroots level. That is what ultimately brings promise to the future.

There is a prayer in the *Book of Common Worship* of the Presbyterian Church-USA and the Cumberland Presbyterian Church (p. 815) that captures the Christian spirit in our relations with the Muslim community. It reads as follows:

> Eternal God, You are the one God to be worshipped by all,
> The One called Allah by your Muslim children, descendants of
> Abraham as we are.

---

5. This point is persuasively argued in Hefling, "How Wide Is God's Mercy?," 22–27.

Give us grace to hear your truth in the teachings of Mohammed, the prophet,
And to show your love as disciples of Jesus Christ, that Christians and Muslims
together may serve you in faith and friendship. Amen.

Faith and Doubt in the Christian Life

The twin subjects of faith and doubt have assumed particular importance for postmodern Christians, and with good reason. In proposing a modest theology for our time I have emphasized two realities that loom large in human existence today: the Mystery of God in this universe that has become unbelievably immense and complex with the more we discover, and the finitude of human beings, limited by time and place and constricted by the cultural worlds that form their thinking and perceiving. In addition, postmodern culture has challenged the rational foundation for philosophical and theological thinking that the modern age assumed, and with it the confidence in reason's capacity to arrive at those ultimate truths that form the substance of Christian theology—the reality of God, the nature of God, the meaning of the incarnation, and so on.

A consequence of this development is that faith has increasingly taken on the character of a Kierkegaardian "leap," an act of risk-taking that the culture may well regard as curious if not foolish. We no longer live in a culture with a convincing sense of the sacred, a culture that is willing to seriously consider theological answers to human questions of meaning and destiny. It is a cultural context in which religious doubt is inescapable for the thoughtful believer, and thus it is not surprising that the subject has drawn considerable attention in our time. In the past, any expression of doubt among the faithful was bound to be an embarrassment, and books addressing the subject typically attempted to alleviate if not remove the embarrassment. Today the approach is quite different. Doubt has become an essential element of a genuine faith.

While this is true, resisting any appearance of doubt remains as a stubborn defense against the threat of losing one's faith. Given the intensely personal nature of doubt, one finds it most directly and often poignantly addressed in novels. Wendell Berry depicts the plight of ministerial student Jayber Crow facing professors who are unable to acknowledge the authenticity of his struggle:

> I went to my professors with my questions, starting with the easiest questions and the talkiest professors. I don't think about them much anymore. I don't hold anything against them. They were decent enough men, according to their lights. The problem was that they'd had no doubts. They had not asked the questions that I was asking and so of course they could not answer them. They told me I needed to have more faith; I needed to believe; I needed to pray; I needed to give up my questioning, which was a sign of weakness of faith.[6]

The issue of doubt raises the question of what faith is all about. We use the word *doubt* primarily in reference to the intellect and to propositions about which we harbor intellectual reservations. We doubt something that doesn't make sense, or seems to contradict what we know for certain. As we noted in chapter 4, however, faith is far more than intellectual assent to certain propositions; it is more than beliefs. Faith in God for the Christian is essentially trust in God that involves the whole person, will and emotions as well as the intellect. We can speak of faith as a deeply rooted commitment, embracing one's whole existence. Nonetheless, Christian faith makes little sense apart from beliefs generated by Scripture and elaborated upon by the church's tradition. They define the content and character of our faith.

When Christians speak of doubts they often are referring to specific teachings that one finds in the theology of their church. They may doubt, for example, that the Bible is inerrant, or that Christ will rule for a millennium at the end of history, even though their church may hold to such beliefs. When we speak of serious doubt for the Christian, however, we have in mind a more fundamental issue, one that addresses more than simply the intellect. We are raising the question whether there is an ultimate meaning to the universe that justifies religious faith; whether our thinking about God actually conveys the reality of God; whether the picture or image of God we encounter in Jesus is a trustworthy revelation of God; whether there will actually be a final consummation to all things that will embrace the human story and "make all things well."

To even raise such questions will likely appear as blasphemy to many Christians, a repudiation of all that identifies us as people of faith. But I believe that raising them can be an act of honesty. There are moments, after all, when we struggle with such thoughts in spite of ourselves, entertaining the possibility that we have been wrong in our convictions. Indeed, to

---

6. Berry, *Jayber Crow*, 52.

acknowledge those thoughts is a more authentic expression of one's faith than to refuse to acknowledge them. This means, as the quote from Guy Collins at the beginning of the chapter suggests, that honest doubt serves the life of faith. It need not compromise one's faith, but rather can instill a humility that is appropriate to the magnitude of what we are confessing as Christians. The poet Christian Wiman offers a wise reflection on the presence of doubt:

> Honest doubt, what I would call devotional doubt, is marked, it seems to me, by three qualities: humility, which makes one's attitude impossible to celebrate; insufficiency, which makes it impossible to rest; and mystery, which continues to tug you upward—or at least outward—even in your lowest moments.[7]

We will differ as Christians in our response to basic convictions of our faith. For me, I am forced to wonder at times about the promise embedded in the gospel itself. Isn't it too good to be true? When one considers the human story, with all of its tragedy, grief, and despair, its senseless violence, cruelty, and bloodshed, how can it all be made right? How can love and reconciliation possibly prevail? We cannot give a rational answer to that question. Nonetheless, the vision of a final consummation in which all things are made right is so meaningful and powerful that for me it compels a "Yes!" in spite of myself. That kind of resolution to the human story and to all of creation would be an ultimate confirmation of the Christian hope and of the life and message of Jesus, who we believe has revealed to us the very heart of God.

While beyond any kind of rational or logical account, this vision fits well with the Christian imagination. That faith-based imagination feeds on the image of a gracious God revealed by Jesus, the God of compassion and mercy in whom we find acceptance, forgiveness, and new life. But our image of God does not stop there; just as it summons us now to a life of faithful discipleship in the way of Jesus, we are told that our lives will be woven into the final consummation as well. "All things will be made new," all things will be transformed, including ourselves. The story of our faith thus arrives at a conclusion that transcends our capacity to know, and that is as it should be. Our lives end in the Mystery that is God, and given what we know in Christ, that conclusion inspires praise and thanksgiving—even in spite of ourselves.

---

7. Wiman, *My Bright Abyss*, 76.

Bibliography

Aslan, Reza. *Zealot: The Life and Times of Jesus of Nazareth.* New York: Random House, 2013.
Aulen, Gustaf. *Christus Victor: An Historical Study of the Three Main Types of the Idea of Atonement.* Translated by A. G. Hebert. New York: Collier, 1986.
Baillie, Donald. *God Was in Christ: An Essay on Incarnation and Atonement.* London: Faber and Faber, 1948.
Baillie, John. *Our Knowledge of God.* New York: Scribner's, 1939.
Barth, Karl. *The Epistle to the Romans.* New York: Oxford University Press, 1968.
Bass, Diana Butler. *Christianity after Religion: The End of Church and the Birth of a New Spiritual Awakening.* New York: HarperOne, 2012.
Beardslee, William. "Christ in the Postmodern Age: Reflections Inspired by Jean-Francois Lyotard." In *Varieties of Postmodern Theology* by David R. Griffin, William A. Beardslee, and Joe Holland, 63-80. Albany, NY: State University of New York Press, 1989.
Berry, Wendell. *Jayber Crow: A Novel.* Berkeley, CA: Counterpoint, 2000.
Borg, Marcus J. *The God We Never Knew.* San Francisco: HarperCollins, 1997.
———. *The Heart of Christianity: Rediscovering a Life of Faith.* New York: HarperOne, 2003.
———. *Jesus: Uncovering the Life, Teachings, and Relevance of a Religious Revolutionary.* San Francisco: HarperCollins, 1989.
———. *Meeting Jesus Again for the First Time.* San Francisco: HarperCollins, 1995.
Borg, Marcus J., and N. T. Wright. *The Meaning of Jesus: Two Visions.* San Francisco: HarperCollins, 1999.
Borgmann, Albert. *Crossing the Postmodern Divide.* Chicago: University of Chicago Press, 1993.
Brauer, Jerald. "A New Paradigm for Theology? Introductory Remarks." In *Paradigm Change in Theology: A Symposium for the Future,* edited by Hans Küng and David Tracy, 205-211. New York: Crossroad, 1989.
Brunner, Emil. *The Christian Doctrine of God: Dogmatics* 1. Translated by Olive Wyon. Philadelphia: Westminster, 1950.
Butler, Christopher. *Postmodernism: A Very Short Introduction.* New York: Oxford University Press, 2002.

Bibliography

Caputo, John D. "Toward a Postmodern Theology of the Cross: Augustine, Heidegger, Derrida." In *Postmodern Philosophy and Christian Thought*, edited by Merold Westphal, 202–28. Bloomington, IN: Indiana University Press, 1999.

———. *What Would Jesus Deconstruct? The Good News of Postmodernism for the Church.* Grand Rapids: Baker Academic, 2007.

Caputo, John D., ed. *Deconstruction in a Nutshell: A Conversation with Jacques Derrida.* New York: Fordham University Press, 1997.

Chittester, Joan. "God Become Infinitely Larger." In *God at 2000*, edited by Marcus J. Borg and Ross Mackenzie, 59–72. Harrisburg, PA: Morehouse, 2000.

Collins, Guy. *Faithful Doubt: The Wisdom of Uncertainty.* Eugene, OR: Cascade, 2014.

Cox, Harvey. *The Future of Faith.* New York: HarperOne, 2009.

Crossan, John Dominic. *The Essential Jesus: Original Sayings and Earliest Images.* New York: HarperCollins, 1994.

———. *The Historical Jesus: the Life of a Mediterranean Jewish Peasant.* San Francisco: HarperCollins, 1991.

———. *In Parables: The Challenge of the Historical Jesus.* New York: Harper & Row, 1973.

———. *Jesus: A Revolutionary Biography.* San Francisco: HarperCollins, 1994.

Delio, Ilia. *The Unbearable Wholeness of Being.* Maryknoll, NY: Orbis, 2013.

Eagleton, Terry. *Reason, Faith, and Revolution: Reflections on the God Debate.* New Haven, CT: Yale University Press, 2009.

Filson, Floyd. *A New Testament History.* Philadelphia: Westminster, 1964.

Franke, John R. *Manifold Witness: The Plurality of Truth.* Nashville: Abingdon, 2009.

Giberson, Karl. "Cosmos from Nothing? Questions at the Edge of Science." *The Christian Century* 132 (June 10, 2015) 20–24.

Green, Garrett. *Imagining God: Theology and the Religious Imagination.* Grand Rapids: Eerdmans, 1989.

Gunton, Colin E. *The Actuality of Atonement: A Study of Metaphor, Rationality, and the Christian Tradition.* Grand Rapids: Eerdmans, 1989.

Hefling, Charles, "How Wide is God's Mercy?" *The Christian Century* 132 (November 11, 2015) 22–27.

Heidegger, Martin. *The Piety of Thinking.* Translated by James G. Hart and John C. Meraldo. Bloomington, IN: Indiana University Press, 1976.

Hyman, Gavin. *The Predicament of Postmodern Theology: Radical Orthodoxy or Nihilist Textualism?* Louisville, KY: Westminster John Knox, 2001.

Johnson, Elizabeth. *She Who Is: The Mystery of God in Feminist Theological Discourse.* New York: Crossroad, 2002.

Johnson, Luke Timothy. *The Creed.* New York: Doubleday, 2003.

Jones, Gareth. *Christian Theology: A Brief Introduction.* Malden, MA: Blackwell, 1999.

Jones, Tony. *The New Christians: Dispatches from the Emergent Frontier.* San Francisco: Jossey-Bass, 2008.

Kierkegaard, Søren. *Concluding Unscientific Postscript.* Translated by David F. Swenson and Walter Lowrie. Princeton, NJ: Princeton University Press, 1944.

Kuhn, Thomas S. *The Structure of Scientific Revolutions.* Chicago: University of Chicago Press, 1970.

Küng, Hans. *Theology for the Third Millennium.* Translated by Peter Heinegg. New York: Doubleday, 1988.

Küng, Hans, and David Tracy, eds. *Paradigm Change in Theology: A Symposium for the Future.* Translated by Margaret Kohl. New York: Crossroad, 1989.

Bibliography

Lose, David J. *Making Sense of the Cross*. Minneapolis: Augsburg Fortress, 2011.
Macquarrie, John. *Jesus Christ in Modern Thought*. Philadelphia: Trinity International, 1990.
Manson, T. W. *The Teaching of Jesus*. New York: Cambridge University Press, 1963.
McFague, Sallie. *Metaphorical Theology: Models of God in Religious Language*. Philadelphia: Fortress, 1982.
McLaren, Brian D. *Everything Must Change*. New York: Thomas Nelson, 2007.
———. *A Generous Orthodoxy*. Grand Rapids: Zondervan, 2004.
———. *A New Kind of Christian: A Tale of Two Friends on a Spiritual Journey*. San Francisco: Jossey-Bass, 2001.
———. *A New Kind of Christianity*. New York: HarperCollins, 2010.
———. *Why Did Jesus, Moses, the Buddha, and Mohammed Cross the Road?* New York: Jericho, 2012.
Merritt, Carol Howard. "Shut up and learn: church in the making." christiancentury.org/blogs/archives/2016-0/most-read articles.
Moltmann, Jürgen. *The Crucified God: The Cross of Christ as the Foundation and Criticism of Christian Theology*. Translated by R. A. Wilson and John Bowden. Minneapolis: Fortress, 2015.
———. *God in Creation: A New Theology of Creation and the Spirit of God*. Minneapolis: Fortress, 1993.
Newbigin, Leslie. *The Gospel in a Pluralist Society*. Grand Rapids: Eerdmans, 1989.
Otto, Rudolf. *The Idea of the Holy*. Translated by John Harvey. New York: Oxford University Press, 1958.
Peacocke, Arthur. *Paths from Science towards God*. Oxford: Oneworld, 2003.
———. *Theology for a Scientific Age: Being and Becoming—Natural, Divine, and Human*. Minneapolis: Fortress, 1993.
Polanyi, Michael. *Personal Knowledge: Towards a Post-critical Philosophy*. Chicago: University of Chicago Press, 1962.
Richardson, Alan. *The Miracle Stories of the Gospels*. London: SCM, 1959.
Ricoeur, Paul. *The Symbolism of Evil*. Boston: Beacon, 1969.
Santmire, H. Paul. *Before Nature: A Christian Spirituality*. Minneapolis: Fortress, 2014.
Sheldrake, Philip. *Spirituality: A Very Short Introduction*. Oxford: Oxford University Press, 2012.
Smith, Huston. *Beyond the Postmodern Mind: The Place of Meaning in a Global Civilization*. 3rd ed. Wheaton, IL: Theosophical, 2003.
Smith, James K. A. *Who's Afraid of Postmodernism?: Taking Derrida, Lyotard, and Foucault to Church*. Grand Rapids: Baker, 2006.
Tanner, Kathryn. *Theories of Culture: A New Agenda for Theology*. Minneapolis: Fortress, 1997.
Taylor, Barbara Brown. *An Altar in the World: A Geography of Faith*. New York: HarperOne, 2009.
Thiselton, Anthony. *Interpreting God and the Postmodern Self*. Grand Rapids: Eerdmans, 1995.
Tickle, Phyllis. *Emergence Christianity: What It Is, Where It Is Going, and Why It Matters*. Grand Rapids: Baker, 2012.
———. *The Great Emergence: How Christianity Is Changing and Why*. Grand Rapids: Baker, 2008.
Tillich, Paul. *Systematic Theology*. Vol. 1. Chicago: University of Chicago Press, 1963.

Bibliography

———. *Theology of Culture*. Edited by Robert C. Kimball. New York: Oxford University Press, 1959.

Updike, John. "The Gospel according to St. Matthew." In *Contemporary Writers on the New Testament Incarnation*, edited by Alfred Corn, 1–11. New York: Viking Penguin, 1990.

Westphal, Merold, ed. *Postmodern Philosophy and Christian Thought*. Bloomington, IN: Indiana University Press, 1999.

Wiman, Christian. *My Bright Abyss*. New York: Farrar, Straus and Giroux, 2011.

Young, Frances M. *Sacrifice and the Death of Christ*. London: SPCK, 1975.

Index

Abelard, Peter, 92–93, 95
analogy, 45n11
Anselm, Saint, 92
anthropic principle, 56
Aquinas, Thomas, *see* Thomas Aquinas
Arius, 64
Aslan, Reza, 73n4
Athanasius, Saint, 84–85
atonement, 92–97
Augustine, Saint, 39, 45, 101
Aulen, Gustaf, 93

Baillie, Donald M., 88–89
Barth, Karl, 4, 38, 52
Bass, Dorothy Butler, 90, 115–16
Beardslee, William, 107
Berry, Wendell, 127–28
Bonhoeffer, Dietrich, 32n4
Borg, Marcus, 42, 80, 87
Borgmann, Albert, xii
Brauer, Jerald, 118
Brunner, Emil, 52n3, 66

Calvin, John, 49, 93
Caputo, John, 11n7, 12, 90
Chittester, Joan, OSB, 38
Christianity, 4–8, 15, 25, 112, 116
church,
    and world religions, 35–36, 118, 122–27
    in pluralistic world, 111–12
    imperial church, 35, 112
    decline of, 115

    necessity of, 119
Collins, Guy, 18, 118
Cox, Harvey, 116
cross, crucifixion, *see* Jesus
Crossan, John Dominic, 74
culture, 1–17

Darwin, Charles, 43
Dawkins, Richard, 40–41
deconstruction, 11–12
Delio, Ilia, 44
Derrida, Jacques, 11–13
Descartes, Rene, 12–13, 20–21
Dyson, Freeman, 55–56

Eagleton, Terry, 40–41
Einstein, Albert, 57
Emergence Christianity, 108–9, 112–14
emergent church, 109–19

faith,
    and imagination, 30–32
    and theology, 32–33, 125
    substance of, 33, 48–49, 62–63, 122, 128
    certainty/uncertainty, 35–36, 52–54
    and doubt, 23, 118, 127–30
Fall, the, 101–2
feminist theology, xi, 47–48
Feuerbach, Ludwig, 61–63
Foucault, Michel, 10–11, 14, 20
Franke, John, 11n5, 27
Freud, Sigmund, 14, 61–63

Index

Fundamentalism, 23, 48, 113–14

Gibson, Mel, 95
God,
   and language, x-xi, 29–32
   of metaphysics, xii, 28, 40, 48, 64
   mystery of, x, 38–39, 43, 127, 129–30
   as love, 42
   as Spirit, 22, 37, 41–42, 44, 47, 63, 66, 76, 88, 126
   existence of, 40–43
   as "Father," 30–31, 47–48, 100
   as human projection, 61–63
   judgment of, 105–6
   "hidden," 49
   evidences of, 51, 55
   Trinity dogma, 63–66
Green, Garrett, 53n4
Gunton, Colin, 45

Hawking, Stephen, 54
heaven and hell, 104–6
Hegel, G.W.F., 15, 49
Heidegger, Martin, 48, 54
hermeneutics, 2, 24–26
   of suspicion, 13–15, 19
Hitchens, Christopher, 40–41
Hyman, Gavin, 10

imagination, xii, 30–32, 44–48, 53
incarnation, *see* Jesus
Intelligent Design, 56
Irenaeus, 4, 66
Islam, 53, 126–27

Jesus,
   of history, 69–72
   the Jews, 74–75n7
   kingdom of God, 73–76
   "wonder works," 76–79
   Son of God, 81–82, 100
   Word (Logos) of God, 82–85, 100
   as God incarnate, 78–80, 83–89
   cross of, 90–97, 102, 104
   resurrection of, 87, 97–101, 106
   and John 14:6, 124–25
Johnson, Elizabeth, 50
Johnson, Luke Timothy, 65–66

Jones, Gareth, 31
Jones, Tony, 109, 112
Josephus, Flavius, 70

Kant, Immanuel, 60
Kierkegaard, Søren, 23, 49, 115, 127
Küng, Hans, 5–7, 21
Kuhn, Thomas, 5

Lessing, Gotthold, 49, 68
literalism, 27, 48, 81, 113
Lose, David J., 93n4
Luther, Martin, 4, 34, 49, 50, 53
Lyotard, Jean-Francois, 11, 15

Macquarrie, John, 98
Marx, Karl, 14
Maurice, F. D., 93–94
McFague, Sallie, xi, 27, 47
McLaren, Brian, 1n2, 74, 106, 110–11, 123
metanarratives, 15–16
metaphorical language, xii, 30–31, 39, 44–48, 81–83, 85–86, 100, 116
metaphysics, x, 24, 28, 32, 39–40, 83–86, 88
modernism, 10, 12, 22–24
Moltmann, Jürgen, 7, 43n7, 103–4n8
mysticism, 59–60

natural theology, 51–54, 58–61
Newbigin, Lesslie, 1, 58n8
Newton, Isaac, 44n8
Nicene Creed, 3, 64–65, 83–84, 86, 88
Nietzsche, Friedrich, 14
nonfoundationalism, 12–13

Otto, Rudolf, 59–60

panentheism, 41
Pascal, Blaise, 25
Paul, Saint (Apostle), 24, 34–35, 41, 53, 63, 87, 98–99, 106
Phillips, J. B., 40n3
Philo of Alexandria, 83n5
pluralism, 16–17, 24–25
Polanyi, Michael, 36
postmodernism/postmodernity,

assumptions, sympathies, xi-xii
representative thinkers, 10–11
language, 12–13
women's movement, 14–15
human nature, 19–20
reason, 12–13, 20–24, 26
theology, xi-xii, 19
Rauschenbusch, Walter, 113
resurrection, *see* Jesus
revelation theology, 52–54
Ricoeur, Paul, 13–14, 102n7

salvation, 101–5
Santmire, H. Paul, 66
Schleiermacher, Friedrich, 5–6, 59
Scripture/Bible, 29, 33, 48, 53, 57, 77, 88, 104–5, 113–14, 124
science,
    vs. religion debate, 40–41
    and religion, 54–58
Sheldrake, Philip, 9, 57–58
sin, 19, 101–3
Smith, James K. A., 10n4, 18
Smith, Huston, 9, 11n8
Spirit, *see* God
spirituality, 120–22
Stott, John R. W., 1

Tanner, Kathryn, 25
Taylor, Barbara Brown, 67–68

Teilhard de Chardin, 44
Tertullian, 77, 84
theism/monotheism, 28, 39–40
theology,
    the laity, ix-x, xii-xiii, 16–17
    culture, 2–7, 112
    relativism, 6–7, 24–25
    dogmatism, 24, 111, 125
    a modest, 23, 27–37, 123
    a hospitable, 35–37
    atheism, 54–55
    a "generous orthodoxy," 111, 114, 119
Thiselton, Anthony, 20
Thomas Aquinas, 31, 45n11, 93
Tickle, Phyllis, 107–8, 113
Tillich, Paul, 42–43, 48, 53, 58–59
Troeltsch, Ernst, 6
truth,
    rational and historical, 22–24,
    possession of, 29, 49, 125
    to know, 87

Updike, John, 67, 74

Westphal, Merold, 19, 23
Wiman, Christian, 99, 129
Wright, N. T., 80, 85

Young, Frances M., 91n3

www.ingramcontent.com/pod-product-compliance
Lightning Source LLC
Chambersburg PA
CBHW022130160426
43197CB00009B/1216